Unscripted

Kaylesa M. Hinsey

TRILOGY CHRISTIAN PUBLISHERS

Tustin, CA

Trilogy Christian Publishers
A Wholly Owned Subsidiary of Trinity Broadcasting Network
2442 Michelle Drive
Tustin, CA 92780

Unscripted

Disclaimer: This is a true story of my lived experiences. Some names and descriptions have been changed to protect privacy.

10 9 8 7 6 5 4 3 2 1

Library of Congress Cataloging-in-Publication Data is available.

ISBN: 979-8-89041-457-1

E-ISBN: 979-8-89041-458-8(ebook)

Dedication

For the lost.

Acknowledgment

I credit this work to the guidance and wisdom of the Holy Spirit that led me out of my comfort zone in the shadows and gave me the desire to be a part of the solution. God has truly been a friend that sticks closer than a brother to me; His presence is always felt whether I am sitting in silence or in a crowded room. I am grateful to Trilogy Publishing for taking a chance on an unknown first-time author who acted on faith and a little courage.

To my family and friends, who always made me feel a sense of belonging and encouraged my independence, thank you. I gained a large part of my spiritual development from my church community, which empowered me with the confidence and humility to do great things in my life. To my godmother, thank you for being a great example and always remembering me.

To my brave sister, your sacrifice will not be forgotten.

Lift Off

The art of a shuttle launching into outer space is captivating and exciting to watch. As it ascends, rocket boosters that help propel the aircraft above the earth detach gracefully as the shuttle disappears from Earth's atmosphere. A launch into a unique environment full of uncertainty and undiscovered possibilities. I imagine the human experience is similar; we leave the comfort of a familiar womb we inhabited for months, detaching from our mother to enter a room filled with new sights and sounds, an experience the brain somehow never remembers. As we grow from infancy to adulthood, our brain collects the information it chooses to reveal or conceal well into maturity until our death. We tend to hold on to good experiences, but somehow, the one thing we never forget is the bad memories, specifically, the first time we experience the feeling of being unseen and misunderstood. It is a guaranteed act that repeats itself throughout our lifetime with heartbreak and abuse of every kind, but God, in His infinite mercy, perpetuates another human experience deep within each of us. The knowledge of His existence. For since the creation of the world, God's invisible qualities—His eternal power and divine nature—have been clearly seen, being understood from what has been made, so that people are without excuse (Romans 1:20, NLT).

As King David expressed,

> If I ascend into heaven, you are there; If I make my bed in hell, behold, You are there. If I take the wings of the morning, And dwell in the uttermost parts of the sea, Even there Your hand shall lead me, And Your right hand shall hold me.
>
> Psalm 139:8–10 (NKJV)

Unlike rocket boosters and an umbilical cord, God's presence is always attached to us. I understood this very early as the unplanned, extremely quiet little girl who always seemed to get picked last growing up. My naïve, undeveloped mind didn't understand why back then, so one day, I climbed to the top of the stairs, sat on the roof of my family's unfinished business, and asked God, "Why did You send me here?" I know it's a strange question for a child to ask; for some reason, I never felt like I fit in, but I always felt God's presence with me, and like most unscripted humans with an uncertain purpose, I made it my mission to never stop searching until I found out. Today is Sunday, my favorite day of the week. As I walked into church confidently around the back, I found a seat in the corner to look for a vacant seat up front. I have come far from the little girl on the roof, but I never left her behind, and now I have the chance to tell the story of how I climbed out of obscurity, a place so many have embraced as their destination in life. This testimony is for the shy, forgotten, misunderstood, abandoned, or unplanned person who has a desire to be seen and heard; you have spent most of your life searching for validation by achieving or choosing to watch life from the sidelines but always longed to get in the game. Those who are or were constantly told you are not talented, pretty, handsome, or good enough; you feel comfortable sitting in the crowd, but you're anointed for a platform. God sees you, and He needs your voice to represent Him. He will use your strength, but it's your weaknesses that advance His grace toward humanity most.

Unscripted: not being planned for or anticipated; said or delivered without a prepared script.

Contents

CHAPTER 1

Orbit: "Why Am I Here?"

"Do not be afraid of those who kill the body but cannot kill the soul. Rather, be afraid of the One who can destroy both soul and body in hell."

Matthew 10:28, NIV

My name is made up of two names; in Hebrew, Kay means "beloved," and Lesa means "consecrated to God." Whether this is true or not, I accept it. Unlike most children, I liked the sound of quiet and lived my childhood inside a room I created in my mind; commonly known as an introvert. It felt safe, and I could create my own little reality to escape the big reality I couldn't understand outside of myself. I am pretty sure any trained psychiatrist has a diagnosis or a few for this behavior, but for me, this was how I chose to survive being misunderstood by myself and the world around me. I am the fourth of five children, and I was a surprise to my parents; born and raised in the Bahamas in a Christian home surrounded by a close-knit, large extended family, which made it very easy for me to get lost and be quiet. When King David was left alone in the field watching his father's sheep as a boy, I imagine he had to learn very important skills of survival to make up for his forgotten state. My family would sometimes remind me that I was so quiet and unbothered as a baby that I rarely cried, and my mother always had to make a special effort to check on me. Normal cries come out with sound, but I was a child that cried silently, whether sad, angry, or afraid. Over time, my inclination was always driven by a voice that arrested my ability to get attention. I embraced the thought that no one needed to rescue me because being by myself never seemed to bother me, so like David and every timid child, I learned the skill of surviving alone quickly. After the space shuttle is launched successfully into space, it begins to orbit. The crew is never alone; the command center is constantly giving instructions and course corrections until the mission is completed. God, our creator, is the personal command center of every human who chooses to acknowledge His existence; therefore, surviving alone is an option, never a requirement.

"Nevertheless I tell you the truth; It is expedient for you that I go away: for if I go not away, the Comforter will not come unto you; but if I depart, I will send him unto you" (John 16:7, KJV).

For those of you who have never been exposed to a Pentecostal church service, you would be shocked to discover that the Holy Spirit is very loud, always excited, dramatic, and can dance better than any famous pop star. At least that's what I thought He was, a performer, and as I got older, I realized my definition wasn't that far off. Jesus described the Holy Spirit as the comforter; He is God's presence within us. The performance of comfort and peace by the Holy Spirit is often overlooked by most and compartmentalized to specific events. As a child, whenever I was left out, not picked, or booted out of a friendship for some reason, I never felt totally alone because I felt God's comfort with me most of the time. I promised myself that one day I would put into words the duality of feeling misunderstood by the world and being seen by God to help those that struggle with hypervigilance and despondency. God promised in His Word that He would never leave or forsake us; He made us all with unique fingerprints and customized DNA and, more importantly, sacrificed His only Son, Jesus, to restore His relationship with us. His love for us is unconditional, infinite, and unyielding; this is why you should never feel like you don't belong. He gave His best just to express how much He values you, which gives you a right to be seen and heard. He wants you to receive that love for yourself and have confidence to live as the unique person you are made to be. It takes a lot of courage to be unique in a world filled with comparison, and the voice of an anonymous group of people called "they" that set the standards for beauty, status, and success in our society. But no matter how hard you try to fit in, there are valuable traits God placed specifically within you that give you a purpose that only you can fulfill.

Among the various gifts God has given me, being quiet and unbothered are my most loved and misunderstood; it projects passivity but also courage and wisdom. In quietness, you can listen, observe, and discern a lot about life, people, and, more importantly, God; it's what fuels my mind with creativity and intuitive knowledge to relate events to stories. The one thing I enjoyed most about being a quiet child was being ignored because it gave me time to imagine and learn, the introvert's dream. Fortunately, my parents decided to give me a younger sister who turned out to be an extrovert, which forced me to come out of my shell from time to time. She was never afraid of a challenge, but I always found a way to go along to get along, which changed when my older siblings relocated, and I became the oldest child in the house. It felt like a nightmare being seen and responsible suddenly. As I look back on that event in my childhood, I am grateful that God didn't allow me to remain hidden because I would have never had the courage to live out or write about a testimony that could save lives.

As a loner, I didn't know how to defend myself, and I experienced different forms of abuse that threatened every stage of my development. I was bullied and treated like a doormat for most of my childhood. Feeling like a mistake most of the time and having an intense fear of people, sexual abuse drove me further into self-isolating behavior to protect my safety and sanity. However, deep down inside, I knew that I was not meant to live life as a victim, and neither were you. The sudden need to defend myself at such a young age forced me to grow up quickly but also helped me discover my right to have a voice in the world as time progressed. I still speak to that little girl inside of me when I remember those frightening experiences from my childhood and let her know she's safe now; I couldn't fully defend myself from irresponsible men, mean girls at school, or verbal abuse, but like so many resilient children, I found hope that one day I would find a way out of silence to advocate for victims of what I survived. Parents, amid your busyness, take time to check in with your children and talk to them about the dark side of life; they need to hear it, especially the less combative, shy ones that often go unnoticed and get lost easily. Give them space in the home to speak up without shame, and don't be afraid to open those doors from time to time where they are locked away for hours on their own. They are hiding for a reason, and they need you to be a part of the safe space God created in all of us.

"Yea, though I walk through the valley of the shadow of death, I will fear no evil: for thou art with me; thy rod and thy staff they comfort me" (Psalm 23:4, KJV).

When I chose my first writing assignment as a personal testimony, I questioned my right to share the difficult and dark parts of my life. I asked God for the courage to be transparent and respectful, afraid of who I might offend or disappoint; then, He reminded me of what it felt like when I wasn't heard and how I used to beg Him to help me understand myself, spending years waiting for someone else to advocate for me. Romans 12:3 (KJV) declares,

> For I say, through the grace given unto me, to every man that is among you, not to think of himself more highly than he ought to think; but to think soberly, according as God hath dealt to every man the measure of faith.

The faith given to each of us by God is measured equally, according to Scripture; I didn't get any less or more but the same amount as every other human being. There will always be someone more talented, accomplished, and beautiful according to the world's standards, but the faith given to each of us levels the playing field. This is a truth I couldn't understand as a child, but during the put-downs, rejection, and abandonment, it was faith that molded me with courage and resilience to embrace the thought that there is no need to silence or lower my voice when it comes to doing the right thing so, slowly, I started using the little wisdom that I learned from being the underdog and watched God multiply it as I got older.

There are laws God created in and around us; if violated, we feel the immediate consequences. If you have a compromised metabolism, eat too much, and lay around all day, you will gain weight. If you walk into traffic, you will be hit by a moving vehicle. But faith is dynamic and the one thing that gives humanity hope beyond reason and logic. Jesus proclaimed that whoever does not receive the kingdom of God like a child shall not enter it. I saw this being acted out one day by my extroverted five-year-old niece. She refused to stop asking the same question until she got a yes answer, no matter how many times I ignored her or said wait. Children have no concept of the word "no" when they know they have a right to something. I promised to treat her to a Disney movie, but in between the spoken promise and the actual event, she broke several rules. Even after I took her game away as punishment the next morning, she woke up as if nothing happened and demanded to see the movie I had promised. She not only assumed she was forgiven but got dressed and told me when it was time to leave. I wish I had that kind of boldness at her age. Having faith to believe God can use you to do great things with your insecurities and failures requires this childlikeness; courage to act on your right to access His promises even when you mess up. Your voice matters. God created you, and you have a right to be seen and heard in the world by giving voice to His truth no matter how much life drags you down.

Throughout history, God called many unqualified people to do His work. Fear is never an excuse. The Bible revealed this truth in the story of Jeremiah, a man with great purpose but many insecurities.

> "Before I formed you in the womb I knew you, before you were born I set you apart; I appointed you as a prophet to the nations." "Alas, Sovereign LORD," I said, "I do not know how to speak; I am too young." But the LORD said to me, "Do not say, 'I am too young.' You must go to everyone I send you to and say whatever I command you.
>
> Jeremiah 1:5–7 (NIV)

You may not be called to be a prophet but called to raise children, drive a bus, or greet people at the door. God's calling is wherever you are today and is preparing you for the future; every step and task has a purpose in it. There is something you possess that you see as insignificant and may have been a burden to you all your life, but it is God's answered prayer to someone praying.

Throughout my childhood, I didn't spend a lot of time speaking but observing how people lived, some carelessly and others responsibly. What I learned is we all have questions that go unanswered but somehow keep on living beyond not knowing what's next, some trusting God's sovereignty and others wandering aimlessly. I didn't allow abuse and rejection to hold me back because I gained an understanding of how the results of silence further promote destructive behavior and give way to the next victim. Those of us equipped with a testimony of recovery but are too afraid to share it limit progress in humanity and may be just as guilty as perpetrators of injustice. But God can change the picture of victimhood you have of yourself into the expressive person He needs you to become for His purpose. He can alter your thinking from "I couldn't be that brave" to helping you see yourself being that brave little by little. It's time to stop letting someone else get in line before you, and when it's your turn, take it even if you're terrified. God always had better plans for me but was patiently waiting for me to do my part, I started by exchanging the safe places I created within myself for His peace and love, and when I did, I discovered that safety isn't perfection or everyone getting along before I act, it isn't always a place of eutopia where it is peaceful and steadiness with no turbulence but sometimes filled with the struggles, pain, and effort involved in progress and change. No matter how cautious we try to frame our path to a dream, someone will get offended, and things will go wrong, but we must keep going. If you have a testimony, talent, or knowledge that can save someone's life, God will help you develop and master it as you share it.

"When my father and my mother forsake me, then the LORD will take me up" (Psalm 27: 10, KJV).

To detach myself from being so guarded and afraid of rejection, God used people and circumstances around me to push me out of my shell. On Sundays, I would always dread the song after the first prayer at church because I knew I would be called on next to read the Scripture. As I walked toward the altar, taking a deep breath and praying, I could pronounce all the words on the pages that fear started to feel normal after a while. It was terrifying, but my parents understood it was a way to get me used to speaking up. I didn't get picked much for anything else, and as time passed, I started to enjoy my name being called for that one thing. It gave me confidence to believe I wasn't meant to be bullied or told I wasn't enough by peers or teachers and gave me the tenacity to overcome the lie that I would always be timid. It's amazing how a small event like that could encourage you to feel a sense of belonging and purpose beyond reason. Everyone has the desire to be acknowledged or called on for something, and that was enough to set me in the right direction. I thank God for the family He chose for me because they didn't allow me to shrink back but didn't expect me to be someone else either; they helped me accept the quiet, unbothered nature as the way God made me. But the world outside me wasn't as kind, and the reality of rejection was a part of life I needed to get used to. Even if it felt like a bitter slow-release pill, I had to learn how to swallow it religiously.

Besides needing to feel acknowledged, the child in all of us needs to feel fully accepted with strengths and weaknesses. David's life in the shadow of his brothers didn't make him a victim. He understood he might have been left out by people but not God; he didn't accept being forgotten as total abandonment; God has placed that feeling within all of us. It's seen in the wonder of nature, our bodies, and our ability to survive impossible odds.

When I was left alone in quietness or isolation, and no one was around, I could feel God's presence when the voice of my parents or siblings was gone, but I didn't know I communicated with Him all the time. Whether you're a child or an adult, He is speaking to your desires and how you are designed and exposing purpose in your insecurities to lead you down the path He prepared explicitly for your life. He is using circumstances and people daily to move you along that right path with and without your cooperation.

Starting high school and adolescence at the same time should be outlawed, but it is usually how life unfolds. With my older siblings gone, I missed the perks of being a younger child where there was always someone older to blame and hide behind. During that part of my life, I focused on academics more than social skills and developed an appreciation for being responsible, working in the family business after school. I would be lying if I said I didn't miss out on being popular, but I was too shy and didn't know how to express my emotions, which made socializing very uncomfortable. I got attention from a lot of boys, but the nerd in me didn't know how to be smart and have a personality at the same time, so I settled for being a wallflower. My parents made education a non-negotiable and top priority in our home but also encouraged us to be leaders and not followers. Managing their small business for those few hours gave me an identity and made up for my impaired social life, but it also gave me a false sense of responsibility and nearly destroyed my health later in life. At home, I never had to be told to sit down, be quiet, and do what was asked more than once, but at school, I usually got picked on from time to time by my teachers for being too quiet, which gave me courage for the next chapter of my life.

Two months after graduation, after my sixteenth birthday, I started my first job and began applying to universities in the United States. At that age, I was too naïve to be trusted to survive in a foreign country on my own, so my godmother helped me get a job as a cashier, which gave me the exposure I needed for the culture shift I would encounter a year later.

> So Jesse had seven of his sons pass before Samuel. But Samuel said to Jesse, "The Lord has not chosen these." Then Samuel said to Jesse, "Are these all the boys?" And he said, "The youngest is still left, but behold, he is tending the sheep." So Samuel said to Jesse, "Send word and bring him; for we will not take our places at the table until he comes here."
>
> 1 Samuel 16:10–11 (NASB)

The comfort of obscurity only lasts for a season if God created you to be out front. David was busy keeping his father's sheep but was chosen by God to be king, a dream he probably never imagined. God has a way of calling on you at the exact time you are content doing your own thing; He knows when a season has ended for you and when another phase should begin. Without warning, He will put you in situations that cultivate the qualities required for the assignment ahead, which usually involves a lot of discomfort. David didn't become king until a decade later, and prior to his ascension to the throne, he had to endure the test of meekness in preparation for his rule. God's rejection of his predecessor Saul made David's training gruesome. As he led Israel to numerous victories in battle, he had to serve a jealous, temperamental Saul to test his humility and ability to serve. As a gifted warrior and musician, he was loved by people in and out of the palace; his people skills were concealed within him despite being raised as a rejected child. He was also very loyal, having several opportunities to overthrow Saul, but instead, he waited on God's timing, serving diligently just as he did as the youngest overlooked member of his family. Doing menial tasks like protecting his father's sheep from predators prepared him as a great fighter; he developed most of his skills in a servant's position.

God's preparation process is intentional. Being left out is not so bad if you're handpicked to do great things. The small things we take for granted help us develop the skills needed for our future. God will cause people who should like you or favor you to reject you to limit their influence, or He may choose others to support you who don't know you but favor you to advance His influence; His ways are far beyond human understanding. Dictionary.com defines meekness as the fact or condition of submissiveness. In the modern world, this is seen as passive and is not welcomed in circles where aggression and self-promotion are applauded. Controlling your strength or power to act and giving way to others requires more discipline than using your strength to have your own way. The Bible says the meek will inherit the earth; people with this character trait have the patience and humility to not only step back and serve but also to lead others gracefully. Having the patience not to rush the process and go through each step is considered old-fashioned and a time waster in our fast-paced society, but I've discovered the more you push against God's timing, the longer the journey takes.

Having the temperament that is never willing to prolong an argument for the sake of being right is not natural to many; it has to be cultivated. Along with shyness, this type of pride needed a bruised ego to work humility into my character. God used the year and a half after high school as life training in the job market to prepare me mentally for university. Working around well-experienced adults opened my eyes to how much help I needed with discipline, submitting to authority, and better social skills to make it on my own for the first time. I went from a pampered adolescent to waking up at 5 a.m. six days a week, working more than forty hours sometimes, stocking the heaviest items in the inventory, serving at a cash register, and bagging groceries; it was a painful welcome to adulthood.

The work environment was like a revolving door. I changed managers frequently, which helped me adjust quickly to different personalities. I enjoyed the job and really missed being a child, but I knew the experience was short-term, so I made the best of it. My parents always taught us to be respectful but never be a pushover; even though I had a quiet temperament, growing up around strong personalities rubbed off on me, and without me knowing, it would surface when I needed it the most. I was still in my country, but after I entered the gates of the naval base, the culture shift was evident, and sadly, it was the first time I experienced discrimination and xenophobia. Customers would place money on the counter when I reached out my hands to collect payments, others wouldn't speak or look me in the eyes, and some of the familiar friendly faces I saw every week would act like they didn't know who I was outside of work. But there were many others who were kind, open, and inclusive, which made me excited about studying in America. My age and college aspirations inspired them to give me a chance to try new things, which exposed me to a level of consumerism I wasn't accustomed to unless I traveled abroad.

During that time, my skill for persuasion surfaced when I was given opportunities to sell high-valued merchandise, a trait I never knew I had but God needed me to develop for use in my future career choice. Having exposure to different cultures socially and being in front of people all the time, I started noticing pressure to improve my image as I attracted more attention. Being teased about weight issues was the norm growing up in my culture and high school, so I didn't bother to change until I saw how other girls my age were admired for being skinny in the culture I was about to enter for the next four years. On my breaks, I would look through magazines, wishing I could be as stylish and thin as the airbrushed images I saw every day, not realizing a seed of deception was being planted as I slowly developed an obsession with weight loss. All those years of being told I was too quiet and being told I would be overweight no matter how hard I tried to be skinny made me want to prove others wrong. At the time, I didn't have the energy to exercise or diet because work consumed most of my time, and filling out college applications was my part-time job. The time to work out my insecurities would come later when I was willing to pay the high cost to be accepted in the college environment.

To uncover our identity, we need to learn how to be content with our skills, personality, and limitations, which means making a lot of mistakes. Not only are those limitations echoed in the condemning voices of name-calling, character deficits, or lies we are told as children that caused us to live in comparisons, but also in the limits within, based on our natural design as an individual. I wasn't blessed with a singing voice or passion for performing, much less model-like height, but I can communicate and write well. Will I ever write an award-winning song or movie script? I don't know, but at that stage, life taught me that homing in on my innate skills would take me further than external beauty ever could. If you asked that young, confused little girl from a small country what she would become, it would not be anything related to serving people, but as someone who willingly went along with God's plan most of my life, anything became possible as I allowed Him to expose me to new ways of thinking that challenged me to find my true self.

CHAPTER 2

Exploration: "Who Am I?"

"John answered and said, A man can receive nothing, except it be given him from heaven."

John 3:27, KJV

At work, my timidity progressively disappeared as I got closer to leaving for college. Being the youngest on staff and most inexperienced, I remember looks of concern as my tenure ended, and I celebrated with family, co-workers, and friends who were both afraid and excited to see me go. Even though I was terrified being out front that year and a half, it was the break I needed to get me out of anti-social behavior and better prepared for my first extended time away from home. At the time, two of my older siblings were already in college, but I decided to attend a different school, tired of being afraid and naïve. So, instead of waiting to be kicked out of the nest, I insanely threw myself into the unknown, where there was no family or friends to hold my hands. Fear of the unknown had become more exciting than scary to me after being exposed to American culture at work, and those terrifying walks to the altar every Sunday made it easier, but nothing prepared me more than being left out. I already felt like I didn't belong most of the time and didn't know much, so I figured the best thing that could happen was to find out where I fit as an individual with little to no direction.

Being raised in a tropical climate, I chose a university in Florida, not too far from home, but I started during spring in forty-four-degree weather cold, lonely, and fearful, which was no comparison to being homesick. The first thing I noticed as I started to socialize was my new peers were far more advanced socially, which meant I had a lot of catching up to do. I also quickly discovered that my island upbringing was both a stigma and delightfully intriguing. Luckily, all freshmen felt a little lost, so it wasn't hard to make friends, and my differences didn't matter much for too long, but I honestly couldn't wait for the semester to start and end. I made great friends but had a very hard time hanging out consistently as I struggled with the weather pattern and culture shift. Fortunately, the openness and diversity of people made me feel safe to experience new things to combat my shyness and introverted nature.

After the shuttle is launched into orbit, exploration begins, which demands keen focus due to the distractions of the new environment outside of Earth. Between studying and socializing, I always had the thought of not letting my parents down and did my best never to fail a class; my shyness was fading a little, but perfectionism was still a problem. I did all the normal things a college student does but never strayed far from my Christian upbringing. It was an anchor that pulled me back when I partied too much, helped me turn down drugs, or whenever I strayed in any direction that threatened my safety.

I went in undecided but quickly found a major after I saw the absorbent tuition fees my parents were paying, not to mention having to survive on the food offered in the cafeteria. I tried out pre-medicine, but after I lost countless nights of sleep studying biology, I did myself and my parents a favor by switching to healthcare management. I have always loved healthcare because I saw so many people around me suffer from illnesses that could be prevented with proper access to information, medicine, and finances, and I wanted to be a part of the solution.

Growing up, we were always exposed to different cultures, ethnicities, and social classes, but studying at a historically black university also helped expand my thinking about how black culture is seen in different parts of the world. Now, living in a culture where the black experience was dramatically different from what I was accustomed to, I realized my perspective was limited. At home, more than ninety percent of our population is black, and discrimination isn't a daily threat to your safety. As I tried to empathize with black culture in my new environment, I struggled to find the same passion for equality and anti-discrimination, but the experiences of racial disparity at work helped me. Eventually, I allowed myself to see life as a black person and not just a black Bahamian by embracing the universal experience of being black without developing any militant beliefs that would cause me to develop hatred. Having an understanding that all men are created equal was tested by the many forms of injustice I read about from studying our history in my formative years, and I thought inequality remained in the past, never expecting to see it in full swing in the present. But I found hope in the faces that looked just like me, rising above the odds by using education to advocate for equality and embrace the freedom established by the generations before us. The desire to understand who I am more deeply was now personal and ancestral, which I think was the most honorable part of my college experience. However, the darker side forced me to confront an identity issue I had carried around for years.

"There are three things that are never satisfied, four that never say, 'Enough!': the grave, the barren womb, land, which is never satisfied with water, and fire, which never says, 'Enough!'" (Proverbs 30:15–16, NIV).

After I completed my first semester that spring, I went back home to my old job with a mind filled with thoughts about being socially inadequate and having doubts about being enough to fit in with my more stylish, sophisticated peers. The seeds of name-calling and body-shaming planted in me as a child had fully matured and begun to manifest in a strict low-calorie diet and extreme exercise regimen that summer. When I returned for the fall semester, I was thirty pounds lighter and finally got the attention and validation I craved, but I still felt extremely empty inside. The compliments and intrigue gave me short-lived confidence as I realized the skinnier me was being liked more than who I really was on the inside, and my happiness turned into sadness. Compromising my health was the least of my worries; nothing was worse than being rejected and overweight. My personality wasn't developed enough to make any highly esteem social club, but I wasn't being ignored anymore, and that made it all worthwhile. In one of my recent Bible study meetings, the question was asked when climbing the ladder of success, how do you know if your ladder is leaning against the wrong building? Someone answered that if you find yourself compromising who you are and what you believe, you're at the wrong building. In our search for recognition and success, compromise often presents us with options to do whatever it takes to get what we want.

At that stage in my life, I just wanted to be seen like every teenager transitioning into adulthood, but when you get comfortable with taking shortcuts in any area of life, your mind becomes tempted to do more and more destructive things to be successful. The university campus being on the highest hill in the city and not having a car gave me the opportunity to do a lot of walking, and even though my parents paid for a meal plan, I only ate cereal that entire semester. I was miserable, but compromise kept asking for more, and I was never satisfied. When I returned home, my appearance was shocking, and jokes turned into concern as I was constantly encouraged to eat, but all I could think about was losing even more weight. I didn't know how to love myself with compassion or unconditionally; being concerned with the opinions of others was more important. Embarrassed and ashamed of myself, I had morphed into the follower my parents always told me not to be, but instead of becoming a victim, I started to explore the healthy side of weight management.

In most of my friendships, I didn't know how to establish healthy boundaries and didn't want to risk rejection, so I went back to spending most of my time alone, and the little connections I had didn't have any room for transparency. I needed to confront my insecurities. To love radically and develop healthy relationships the way God intended requires vulnerability, being honest about yourself and your feelings, and assuming the risk of being hurt is the only way to experience authentic love. With the assistance of the Holy Spirit and some tough love, I eventually discovered the kind of love I needed to face my low self-worth and body image issues. My primary love languages are acts of service and quality time, but because I struggled with people-pleasing, I experienced repetitive cycles of one-sided relationships by not allowing myself to be valued more than the things I could offer. It would take me years of weight fluctuations, failed relationships, and health issues to realize how badly I needed internal healing, not just for myself but the people God needed me to reach in the future. I tried to convince myself that external accomplishment was what God needed from me, but it was the intangible pain that people couldn't see that He used to give me purpose. As I experienced persistent internal misery, the pressure to remain silent became too overwhelming, and I started journaling habitually. As I accepted the path to rediscover my voice, I took back ownership of my life, and my opinion of myself changed progressively into the person I always knew existed. There is a space inside every willing heart that answers the call to follow God-given desires, and adversity has a way of pushing us toward them at the right time.

"For the earth bringeth forth fruit of herself; first the blade, then the ear, after that the full corn in the ear" (Mark 4:28, KJV).

Ambition and pride drove me to become more of a risk-taker throughout my life, specifically throughout my twenties. During that phase in my life, I was immune to what-ifs, and being uncomfortable was hidden in my subconscious, but as I matured, the anesthetic wore off, and everything seemed harder. Besides physical discomfort, faith became more uncomfortable, and transitions got longer.

While I was shopping one day, God led me to buy a pair of stilettos. I liked the style, but they were very uncomfortable. I thought, *Lord, where am I going to wear these shoes?* The more I got the feeling of putting them back, the louder the prompting to purchase them became, so I bought them. At that point in my life, I was transitioning into a more submissive mindset in my relationship with God. The next morning, during my prayer and meditation time, while I was thinking about how comfortable and safe my life felt, God set my eyes on those shoes. He began to reveal how my unwillingness to be uncomfortable in areas of my life where I fell short, lacked confidence, and gave up frequently continued to keep me safe but stagnant. The pandemic was ending, and I was relieved that some normalcy had returned, but the world had changed in a very uncomfortable way, and more discomfort was the last thing on my mind. I also saw the level of effort required to achieve the glamour and height of success in those shoes, which I had lost the energy and drive for over time. I had dreams of doing something great for God, and His question to me was how far I was willing to walk in discomfort to get to the places where He needed me. He then showed me the times I struggled to pursue jobs, degrees, and relationships successfully without fear of people's opinions or lack of resources to restore my confidence. I always had an affinity to ignore being uncomfortable, not getting picked, or losing when I went after a goal. I almost never shied away from taking the long, narrow path, and this was God's way of telling me to get back to work.

We all have a coward who speaks to us when life gets exhausting; it tells us to live in the comfort of excuses, but a faithful heart is always ready to embrace whatever it takes to complete the assignments. Becoming more and more uncomfortable being a follower in areas God needed me to lead, I ended passivity and allowed writing to keep me grounded every time I felt unstable. Finding my voice on paper helped me understand myself and saved my life, and even though I didn't have the courage then to publish anything, I believed someday God would make good use of it. Today, I can happily say I no longer struggle with extreme diets and exercise, but it wasn't easy. Body image issues can extend well into adulthood and take persistent inner healing work to resolve, especially if they are attached to childhood trauma. I am learning to love my body at any size and unlearning the habit of devaluing myself when I feel inadequate; I only wish I knew then what I know now.

> And what union can there be between God's temple and idols? For we are the temple of the living God. As God said: "I will live in them and walk among them. I will be their God, and they will be my people. Therefore, come out from among unbelievers, and separate yourselves from them, says the LORD. Don't touch their filthy things, and I will welcome you."
>
> 2 Corinthians 6:16–17 (NLT)

When I thought of an idol as a child, I envisioned an image or object that people worship, but anything can become an idol if you place it where God should be in your life: your mate, career, children, food, sex, accomplishments, beauty; the list is endless. As I moved from a wide-eyed freshman to a seasoned senior, my idol was being independent; self-sufficiency was a goal I thought everyone needed to have in life. I was a good

Christian girl part-time, but my full-time job was making sure I always had enough education, charisma, wit, and resources to take care of myself. The hierarchy of my life from top to bottom was myself, my career, money, family, and then God; the reverse was never an option for me because I could only trust myself. The first time I realized I couldn't manage life independently from God was during the last semester of college. I wanted to stay in the United States, establish a great career, and live as far away from home as possible. I begged God to go along with my plan because I did not want to go back home to my parent's house with no job, but no matter how much I cried, the flight was booked, and my old bedroom was waiting for me. After experiencing four years of freedom, I ended up back in my parent's house with a degree, a bruised ego, and too many shoes; when it got quiet, and there was no more fast-paced college life surrounding me, I started to hear this overpowering sound like a knocking on my heart as I unpacked. Instead of listening, I complained, cried, and tried to sleep the pain of disappointment away for months. Suddenly, those feelings of not being chosen returned, and I didn't know what to do with them. Every time I tried to block them out, the Holy Spirit prompted me to stop running and face the pain of not wanting to be seen; I thought my problem was people's disapproval, but my deepest rejection and abandonment issues were self-inflicted. I found myself asking God the same question night after night, "Why did You send me back here?" It was time to grow up, but I wasn't ready, so I was back in the nest, having to take a job. I was overqualified for the next two years to help bring me to the end of myself.

I needed a humbling experience to help me let go of my false persona of having it all together; instead of being a sophisticated executive in a busy city with a thriving social life, I was offered Sunday school teacher at the local Baptist church on an island. God had finally gotten me to a place where my assignment would be to find identity in Him. It was also His way of letting me know that degrees, image, and reputation alone would not qualify me for the life He had prepared for me. I didn't need to discover my worth but reclaim it, and the best place to do it was where all the unresolved pain of my past existed.

Being misinformed, I didn't know His guidance was required to navigate every aspect of my life. I thought my free will meant more than His sovereignty, and I only needed to consult with Him in case of emergency. How we show up in the world matters. I thought my ability and gifts would get me whatever I desired in life, but I learned very quickly that life only worked that way outside of God's system. As I began observing people with far less go farther and faster with God, I wondered what I had to do for that kind of favor but didn't know how to ask for help.

Last night, I had a dream; I was shopping again, but this time, I was given free perfumes and cosmetics. Out of nowhere, a bully from my childhood appeared and tried to befriend me as an adult. Feeling sorry that she wasn't given anything, I offered one of the items, and she chose the perfume I wanted the most. After letting her have it, I went back to the store asking to purchase the same item, thinking how valuable it must be, only to be told it cost four bucks. Most things that are free in life have little value, are easier to let go, and depreciate quickly. When we take the easier route and choose what is mostly free or inexpensive, the respect for that thing or opportunity is never comparable to something we worked hard to achieve. God takes us on some difficult paths to understand this in our relationship with Him, but He will never ask us to give up anything that is more expensive than His replacement. Losing my idol of independence meant gaining a life depending on God and community, the way He designed us to live. There is nothing wrong with wanting a career or success; He just wants to be part of shaping your character to sustain the path.

After I applied for jobs in the city relentlessly, I finally got the break that gave me what I cherished most: my independence. By that time, the Holy Spirit had already started the process of repairing several broken areas in my heart. During those two years I spent at home in my parents' house, every morning before I went to work, I watched Christian television and attended church every Sunday. When I arrived in the city to an apartment of my own with no roommates or family, it was exciting for a few weeks; I had regained the freedom I lost temporarily. But then the reality of adulthood set in; for the first time in my life, I had to pay my own bills and manage my own safety, which deepened my depression. The simple luxury of having someone to talk to at home every day made independence more of a burden than freedom. To escape, I started relying more on nightclub hopping on the weekends, shopping, or any social activity just to not be at home alone for long periods of time.

Living alone wasn't as sexy as I thought; the transition to city life forced me to face many lies as I continued to keep people and God at a safe distance. To toughen up quickly, I thought socializing with my extroverted friends was the best way to lose my timid demeanor, but after that lifestyle became too exhausting for my introverted nature, I turned back to the church and got baptized. I didn't fully understand what baptism meant, but I did notice something had changed when I didn't have the desire to run from my problems anymore. I couldn't listen to the same music without feeling wrong, I lost my attraction to guys who didn't honor God, and I finally gave up pretending to like alcohol, which was the best part. The imposter in me was already dead; pretending to hold on to her was miserable. There were no more disappearing acts in me; I was ready to do the hard, progressive work of change. The truth is, long after cuts and bruises turn into scars, some of our physical attachment to trauma remains, and recovery takes a lot of discipline, self-awareness, and asking for help.

As soon as I slowed down, the consequences of my bad decisions from my past surfaced. Two years prior to my move, I broke up with a guy that became very controlling and obsessive; we met on one of my summer breaks from college. His extreme interest in me made me feel seen, so I overlooked all the red flags about his character as he pursued me. And I foolishly let him back into my life to feel the high of his attention again, but for the next year, I found myself being stalked and slandered relentlessly. As my hypervigilance increased, I thought I would calm down eventually, and no professional help was required. Night after night, I found myself waking up from nightmares and losing sleep; this wasn't the first time my safety was threatened. The little girl who suffered abuse and managed to escape the rooms she was hidden in by sexual predators was still waiting to be rescued from the effects of trauma; she was sitting awake with me years later, just as frightened.

After those incidents, more fears from my past resurfaced. I thought that surviving trauma would be my way of life forever and accepted it moving forward, mostly with a self-isolating routine from work to home and church. The enemy wreaked havoc on my mind day and night as I continued avoiding the need to talk to someone about my inner pain. Until I had a dream that shook me out of my despondency. In the dream, I saw myself sleeping as an evil appearance stood at the foot of my bed with three large stones in a triangle form in his chest. As he reached in to launch one of the stones at me, I stopped him by speaking the Word of God out loud. At the time, I was attending a Pentecostal church, which helped me understand the spiritual realm better as I passively watched the Word of God spoken by the congregation every Sunday. Knowing my life of silence was doing more harm than good, the Holy Spirit opened my eyes to the dark side of the spiritual world and guided me to the solution in God's Word.

I was a simplistic Christian who attended church and boasted about my relationship with God but ignored speaking His Word with conviction and didn't know how to rely on His strength to carry it out. If I had not made the spoken Word of God through teaching and declarations a daily habit, anxiety and depression would have consumed my life, and my testimony would be hidden in an epitaph. Satan's sole purpose is to destroy God's good plans for every life through whatever is idolized most, and he uses good things and bad things. If you hold on to the need to keep whatever feels like freedom, you'll remain imprisoned. The journey is never easy. The words of Mark 4:28 motivate us to keep going, taking one step at a time on the way to our freedom.

A holding pattern is used to keep an aircraft in protected airspace while delaying its arrival at a later point along its route.[1]

Learning new boundaries without becoming overly aggressive or cynical as I adjusted to city life was a daily task. The noise, congested traffic, and stress took some time to get used to, but I was determined to hold onto my gentle nature, refusing to let the external challenges keep me in a holding pattern of hypervigilance. During my travel to New York, air traffic control had my flight, along with several others, in a holding pattern due to congested runways. As I looked out the window at other aircrafts, wondering how much fuel we had left, my anxiety subsided a little as I realized we were not alone in that temporary setback and would be cleared to land eventually. Holding patterns happen to us throughout life; some keep us safe from harm while others prevent us from moving forward, but we should never make them our home and always remember we are not alone in our experiences.

1 Pilot Institute. "How to Fly in a Holding Pattern." Pilot Institute, April 26, 2022. https://pilotinstitute.com/holding-patterns/.

During the year I was stalked and harassed, I regret letting myself be victimized for having the right to reject a relationship I no longer wanted. As an adult, it was the first time my "no" was opposed aggressively, and confronting him directly wasn't an option. Bullies don't remain on the playground; they eventually become entitled adults with poor boundaries. In the story of Jacob, Leah, and Rachel depicted in the book of Genesis, my heart grieved for Leah and Jacob, who were both demoralized by unrequited love for years. Their story teaches us the patience required to love and the struggle we encounter when we demand our own way. It's a picture of God's compassion toward the unloved, less chosen, and those who manipulate their way through life. Imagine having to watch the person you love long for someone else, and the more you try to be seen by them, the further you push them away. When we don't get the things that we crave desperately in life, the disappointment keeps us close to God's plan and purpose. He doesn't create delays to hurt us; we live in an imperfect world. His plans are perfect; these holding patterns are often consequences of insecurities we have within ourselves that we choose to protect and project versus confront and let go. God's love is filled with freedom and void of threats and mind games; it is a necessary part of our free will, which means rejection cannot be eliminated from the selection process.

I think God made the risk of rejection a part of the process to challenge the motives of the heart. Love is never in a rush; this is reflected in Jacob's love for Rachel, as he was willing to serve her deceptive father for years just to have her. Love also makes unpleasant requests like pray for your enemy, be gracious to those who mistreat you, and assume the best when the worst keeps happening. Loving God's way takes a lot of courage, but when the purity of His love enters your heart, any fear of rejection and abandonment within lose potency as you find it easier to let go of what is not meant to be and begin to assume accountability for the real issues within you. Jacob had been deceptive toward his brother, and he needed to learn what love really meant in the practical sense. God's way of justice is getting you to see and feel the hurt you inflicted on others to convict you to choose better. We become more impactful when we accept the lessons that come with our failures and disappointments. To begin uncovering who we really are includes surrendering areas of shame and hurt; no amount of church attendance, partying, titles, awards, or money will satisfy the part of you that needs spiritual healing; we do it for ourselves and the people we love.

My mother led me to the Lord as a child after I woke her from a nightmare about the end of the world (yes, I dream a lot); earlier that day, I read a newspaper article about assumptions that heaven was located within a newly discovered black hole in outer space. In the dream, all I could remember was seeing the four horsemen of the apocalypse, which would be enough to scare any child out of hell. When I rededicated my life to Christ, I felt the light of God open my heart and mind to a world of pain I was ignoring and providential relationships designed to make my life easier. The Holy Spirit reminded me of these specific dreams to reveal why my mind was constantly being attacked with fear to keep me silent and away from my purpose; the answer to who I am was hidden behind all the things I called weak within myself. The presence of God helps us function as we work through our dysfunction, but it is not where God wants us to remain. What we see as trash, He redeems as treasure. You may not have a large circle of friends, and people may not notice your potential, but always assume that God's best is available to you. And His best will always be His love for you. Despite any wrong you've done, He approves of you. For some reason, God loves the underdog, the one that is "available" and working in the background comfortably, whether by choice or circumstance. He loves the tender eyes of Leah and deceptive Jacob, which is good news for all who accept their imperfections.

A year and a half after I moved to the city, I was laid off and found myself unemployed for the first time in my career, with only three months of income to survive. I didn't have much time to cry, so I took a job in life insurance sales for the next year, which I was surprisingly good at, and even though I won awards, I hated it thoroughly. Trying to work through the depression and embarrassment of being fired from a job I prayed for desperately wasn't easy. I used most of my breaks to cry in the bathroom, which help me function emotionally during that time. While I was studying in the United States, I was rejected for a job in pharmaceutical sales, and miraculously, a position in the Caribbean market became available with the same company. By that time, I was already used to being rejected daily in the sales environment, so I took a chance, applied, and after a year of taking trips to the last stall in the ladies' room, my crying sessions ended. In the middle of the post-9/11 era, I found myself in airports, flying throughout the Caribbean and loving it. I was never comfortable being tied to a desk, but I didn't know where I belonged until God got me there the hard way. During my tenure, I learned a lot about medicine and the body, but the most important thing God needed me to understand was the value of having people in my life to help me mature through teamwork.

Being a self-proclaimed loner, I was getting into a lot of trouble developing habitual transactional connections, thinking I was looking out for myself. This self-preservation attitude had gotten me through my childhood with minimal damage but didn't work well in my adulthood. Group dynamics was scary to me; it made me very uncomfortable because it meant I had to be vulnerable and share myself, which revealed my social deficits due to my lack of close connection with God and others. Despite my academic qualifications, my communication skills needed some help, and my introverted nature made the process physically challenging as I found myself having to shut down like a drained battery from the social demands of being in a group. To gain more control of my emotions, I finally gave in and went to therapy to understand myself and how to show up better in relationships. Giving up my fear of being judged, I started to view talk therapy in a more positive light; it was one of the best decisions I made in the process of uncovering who I was as an individual. It is much easier to get along with people when you understand yourself and can communicate with confidence. Outside of my relationship with God, investing in therapy helps me to do life better consistently.

> Then the Lord said [to Jonah], "You had compassion on the plant for which you did not work and which you did not cause to grow, which came up overnight and perished overnight.

> Should I not have compassion on Nineveh, the great city in which there are more than 120,000 persons who do not know the difference between their right and left hand, as well as animals?"
>
> Jonah 4:10–11 (NASB)

When God took away the plant He provided for Jonah during his pity party, He was asking him to question the higher value he placed on getting justice more than having compassion for the innocent lives of Nineveh, who needed redemption to escape judgment. He gave me my dream job to get me to a place where I could see the value of facing my inner pain for myself and, more so, others. The journey was for a testimony, and just like He did with Jonah, He took away my comfort of being silent by allowing a storm every time I attempted to retreat to self-pity.

Emotional intelligence (EI), also known as emotional quotient (EQ) and emotional competence, is described as the ability to recognize, interpret, and manage emotions in oneself and others. As I became more self-aware, I have simplified emotional intelligence as knowing where you begin and end in relation to others. Growing up with strong-willed, emotionally stable influences helped shape my ability to be aware of my emotions, but instead of expressing them, I internalized them. When you are emotionally insecure and hold on to unresolved trauma, circumstances that are considered normal affect you differently than those that are emotionally mature; it's very hard to have an even temperament when you don't practice validating your own emotions. You become easily offended by trivial situations repeatedly and don't know how to change; you are temperamental one day and on cloud nine the other; it is an exhausting way to live. To further complicate the issue, you find it hard to concentrate when you need to make rational decisions. I was obligated to stay abreast of clinical updates, study new drugs, and monitor competitor activity daily, but my ego convinced me to keep adding more cognitive demands to my mind by pursuing MBA studies. While ambition is good, it is vital to have the capacity to execute our goals at a healthy pace. By that time, I realized I had bit off more than I could chew; my body had hit a wall, and a weakening immunity caused me to develop multiple health issues. If I had only learned to allow my emotions to settle and thought out a more realistic timeline to achieve my goals, I would have avoided those problems.

One night, I woke up with a sharp, paralyzing pain in my back from a hairline fracture; I was so frighted I didn't even think about calling anyone but drove myself to the emergency room doubled over in pain. Another time, I was bedridden with the flu for two weeks, fractured my toe the next, and the list kept piling up, but I refused to stop going. Fortunately, I had a healthy group of people in therapy that helped me learn to manage my emotions and rational thinking progressively. After I got over my acute physical sick streak, I started having severe pain in my eyes that made it hard to focus. At first, I thought I just needed glasses, but as the pain persisted, I knew something was terribly wrong. I had just put a down payment on a house and was wrapping up grad school. During a visit with my optometrist, as he checked my eye pressure again and again to make sure he was getting the right readings, I instinctively knew I was in trouble. The next words I heard changed my life in an instant, and this time, the problem wasn't acute but chronic.

Before my diagnosis, I was living a relatively self-sufficient, all-about-me life; I liked being a Christian in theory, but now I would develop a clearer understanding of what it meant practically. I was okay not actively seeking God daily as I should; ambition moved Him out of every aspect of my life, and I only invited Him in on major issues, but this time, I didn't want to figure things out for myself with my eyesight being threatened; my life was severely out of control. That night, I was so afraid to close my eyes; all I could think about was seeing darkness for the rest of my life in one moment and then quickly coming up with things I needed to do to prepare myself in the next. The unfortunate irony of my diagnosis was that I was busy promoting the same products I would have to depend on for the rest of my life; I walked in and out of clinics, hospitals, and pharmacies explaining the importance of getting your eye pressure checked regularly, but never considered checking my own. As a child, I developed a habit of going into survival mode whenever I experienced a moment of crisis by not allowing myself to feel the pain until I couldn't hold it inside any longer. I didn't have time to allow fear to overtake me because I was living alone, had a career, a pending mortgage, and other obligations to manage, so instead of sinking into fear, I allowed the diagnosis to give me purpose to live with more intention and start embracing the imperfect sides of myself. I learned to adapt quickly from watching my parents and grandparents honor commitments no matter how difficult life got, and I expected nothing less from myself. After I filled my prescriptions and embraced my new way of life, I thought things couldn't get any worse, but my life was about to get more interesting.

The grace I had for the fast-paced life I was living was over, but I refused to do what I knew was necessary to readjust by finding a less demanding job. I continued working until my manager added a new drug to my portfolio that required a two-week study and exam, then a rigorous promotional campaign. As I sat at my desk, looking at an encyclopedia-sized module, tears began to flow from my eyes; it was time to appropriate my values and straighten out my life. I was empty physically and emotionally; there was nothing left. The dreams I had were happening, but I was burnt out. So, I gave myself permission to get lost for a while and surrendered the workaholic that made little room for God, that was losing her health, and had ruined most of her intimate relationships; I was spending a lot of money on doctors, my life was consumed with darkness, and I needed to find the light again. If I had sum up my resolve at that point in my life, it would be a quote from Marcus Aurelius, "It is not death that a man should fear, but he should fear not beginning to live." The voice that kept warning me to stop overextending myself was now looking over my shoulders as I wrote my resignation letter, turned it in, and walked away from certainty to enter one of the most liberating periods of my life, and I was happy to embrace it.

CHAPTER 3

Abort Mission: "Growing Pains"

Come to me, all you who are weary and burdened, and I will give you rest. Take my yoke upon you and learn from me, for I am gentle and humble in heart, and you will find rest for your souls. For my yoke is easy and my burden is light.

Matthew 11:28–30 (NIV)

I always thought the rest Jesus offered was primarily physical, but as adversity continued to erode my spiritual and emotional peace, my desire for rest internally became more imperative. The kind of peace where I didn't need to have it all together to be accepted or strive to achieve anything. I always admired the courage and humility in people who knew they didn't fit in but showed up anyway. People who walked away from careers that made them miserable and traded suits for jeans and t-shirts; it's a heroic response to the "enough" signal life gives to overworked bodies and minds that can no longer tolerate existing and start living. At this stage, there is no more listening to peoples' disapproval about how to dress, walk, or talk; we stop getting ready and accept the different assignment life is calling us to carelessly. I think this is one of the reasons God chooses the eccentrics like John the Baptist, who wore camel hair and ate a diet of grasshopper and honey for radical assignments; John was probably one of the most confident and misunderstood people that walked the planet during his time.

I grew up believing strongly that flaws had to be fixed or concealed to make it anywhere great in life, especially in God's kingdom, but starting from the bottom again shifted my thinking dramatically. NASA describes a black hole as a region in space where the pulling force of gravity is so strong that light is not able to escape. There are places and times when coping with the stress of life becomes overbearing, and the fight goes out of you, where sadness, disappointment, and exhaustion consume you to a breaking point, and hope is lost. Quitting was seen as cowardly and selfish to many, but when I was forced on a sabbatical from my career-driven life to face my declining health, how I looked to people became irrelevant.

Growing up with a strong religious upbringing, mental health was given little attention; the common advice was to keep it private and be strong. I still don't understand why diseases of the brain are more stigmatized than other organs of the body when it is the mind that guides our decisions and how we serve God; our minds should be treated as our most expensive asset. When I kept experiencing loss, no matter how hard I worked or tried to make an impression, my life began to drift slowly into a dark but comfortable place where being weak was okay, and, to be honest, it felt good, at least temporarily. The pressure to be perfect was leaving me, and I was happy to start the process of saying goodbye to my imposter. Because light cannot escape black holes, they are invisible; however, space telescopes with special instruments can help find them. There is no escaping the presence of the Lord if you belong to Him; He goes with you in those very low places where you think no one is watching.

During my neuroscience studies in pharmaceutical sales, I had to learn about the brain and its center of emotions, the amygdala and limbic system, whose primary role is processing memory, decision-making, and emotional responses (including fear, anxiety, and aggression). It's the place in your brain that helps you decide what you can and cannot handle emotionally. Unfortunately, because we live in an imperfect world where circumstances have become increasingly unpredictable and fast-paced, emotional imbalances occur often. God made the human mind and body adaptable, but when our reaction to trauma is misappropriated by frequency and intensity, sometimes our flight instead of fight responses take over, and it can take us longer to restore balance and move on with our lives. Despondency was a comfortable place for me, having overworked my intelligence while repressing my emotions for a prolonged period. Up to that time in my life, a black hole was what I needed; it was the first time I didn't have something to wake up for or a project to finish based on my extreme timeline. No one was calling for a favor, I had no errands to run, and my time was filled with exploration again, so I put my bag of chips down, got dressed, and started volunteering until I found another job.

Romans 8:26 (KJV) says, "Likewise the Spirit also helpeth our infirmities: for we know not what we should pray for as we ought: but the Spirit itself maketh intercession for us with groanings which cannot be uttered." Even though fear from trauma was attacking my mind, I didn't allow it to ruin my newfound freedom of not having a full-time job. It was God's Spirit that woke me up to practice fighting instead of fleeing every morning. Somedays, my body was so tired I wanted to stay in bed and forget everything; it was important to let myself be numb for a while, but only a while. Thankfully, the Word of God had entered my heart and already taken root to help me confront the harsh reality of starting over. Jesus said the kingdom of God is like a man that scatters seed on the ground night and day; whether he sleeps or gets up, the seed sprouts and grows, though he does not know how.

The year prior to these catastrophic events, I had completed a year in therapy and surrounded myself with people living a more spirit-filled life. A Sunday before my resignation, we started a biblical declaration challenge. Biblical declarations are words spoken over specific areas of life based on God's promises. What was meant to be a daily challenge for a few months turned into a lifestyle for me; it prepared me for the future and helped me dispel a few myths from my past. The first stronghold I had to fight was depression, which was at its worst when I heard my neighbors leaving for work every morning; research has proven that the most practical way to confront sadness is to get into a routine. Every morning, I woke up, read my declarations, sent out resumes, cried, ate, slept, and then got depressed all over again when I heard the neighbors returning home from work; it was an imperfectly balanced routine. After I got tired of the four walls of my apartment, I decided to volunteer at marketing firms to keep myself out of the house until I found a permanent job. Having been employed most of my adult life, I didn't know how to sit still for too long.

One day, the owner of the firm showed me an ad for a sales position at an international company. Knowing I was overqualified for the work I was doing, she insisted that I apply for the job immediately, and I did, but I never expected a response. When I got the call, I was told the application process for the position was already closed, but after my application was reviewed, they decided to reopen it. The resilient character trait that was cultivated from years of pushing through difficulty, along with the Word of God, forced me out of my pity party just in time. Time and chance had been calling me all my life, and I was used to answering. I had to make the decision to take back control of my life by standing on my faith and ignoring my feelings.

When I applied for the job, I was right on the verge of losing my apartment due to my depleted savings; acting on something is always better than doing nothing. The Spirit of God is meeting you in the middle of despondency, where the gravity of failure is trying to destroy your reason to hope, and it seems like goodness will never return, and that is when you need to get up and fight the most. After a series of panel interviews, I was hired. I never felt like saying those declarations, but I did every morning as a way of prophesying my future, defeating my past, and inviting God's promises into my present circumstances. Many of my prayers were answered by a person or people that I didn't know that well and never would have crossed paths with if I had remained idle and accepted defeat. It's okay to have bad feelings, but never let it arrest your ability to act and remain in motion; rest for a while, but never get too comfortable. God is with you, and He wants to get you to the provisions.

> When Elijah heard it [God's voice], he pulled his cloak over his face and went out and stood at the mouth of the cave. Then a voice said to him, "What are you doing here, Elijah?" He replied, "I have been very zealous for the LORD God Almighty. The Israelites have rejected your covenant, torn down your altars, and put your prophets to death with the sword. I am the only one left, and now they are trying to kill me too."
>
> 1 Kings 19:13–14 (NIV)

Depression affects over 280 million people worldwide, but because mental health issues are still commonly viewed as a stigma, it is often undiagnosed and untreated; the hopelessness Elijah felt is a daily reality for many people. Depression does not discriminate. It is multidimensional and can manifest from persistent adverse circumstances, chemical imbalances, physical illness, environmental causes, or spiritual attacks. The treatment approach can look different for everyone, which is why it is very important to consult a trained health professional, counselor, or pastor to guide you. Addressing the issue only on a physical level made me suffer unnecessarily for years, but as I searched for biblical solutions and entered therapy to help me process my emotions in healthier ways, my healing journey became easier. I experienced a calmer and more peaceful life when I decided to use a community-based approach to heal from issues that made my life difficult; it was scary, but continuing to live in defeat was far worse. James 5:15–16 (NIV) says,

> And the prayer offered in faith will make the sick person well; the Lord will raise them up. If they have sinned, they will be forgiven. Therefore, confess your sins to each other and pray for each other so that you may be healed. The prayer of a righteous person is powerful and effective.

Prayer became my first line of defense, and then I added confession, for example, therapy, biblical declarations, and church small group to break down my lingering internal insecurities. We often have an easy time with prayer, but confessing our faults and struggles to others is more difficult. Taking the steps to get over my shame and pride by starting therapy meant going beyond church attendance; I had to sacrifice some finances, but it was worth it. There are countless people who struggle Sunday after Sunday, hoping the solution to their internal pain will miraculously appear without having to do anything but pray. I know because I was one of them. I didn't find out until a few years later that the root of my depression symptoms was both physical and mental. To become employed again, I couldn't stay inside hoping a job would come to me; I had to drop my pride and go outside and network with people who were already employed. This same principle holds true in other areas of your life; you must approach the problem internally and become externally motivated to do whatever it takes to heal.

God wants us to enjoy the freedom and happiness He promised in His Word. Throughout the journey, the more I shared my imperfections with proper discernment, the lighter I became. As I connected with people who had already experienced breakthroughs or were going through similar situations, the process of healing was not only easier but faster. Give your body, mind, and soul the freedom it is asking for, commit to doing the hard work of relying on God's strength daily to get out of bed, put one foot on the ground, then the other, walk to the bathroom, brush your teeth, take a shower, get dressed, and eventually, you'll find your way out the door. This may sound trivial to someone who has never felt the hopelessness that accompanies depressive episodes, but having a simple routine is what helps you recover progressively. I had to practice saying, "God will help me face this day," every time I wanted to give up. He sent Jonah a plant and sent Elijah a raven, and He sent me strength for my senses to hear the sermons and say the prayers that surpassed understanding. Whenever the awful feelings of depression and anxiety persisted, I became just as persistent in pushing past the hopelessness, seeing it as more practice doing difficult things for wherever God was taking me, which prepared me for my next assignment. As I entered my new job assignment in logistics, I was equipped with the wisdom needed to adapt to a larger reach of customers with greater responsibility and the stress of a faster-paced industry.

"If anyone serves me, he must follow me; and where I am, there will my servant be also. If anyone serves me, the Father will honor him" (John 12:26, ESV).

When God puts a vision in your heart, living intentionally becomes a way of life; there will be things that the people surrounding you can do that you can't, you will be forced to wait through difficult and impossible odds, you will be criticized, the finances will not be there, your health may be attacked, and you will spend a considerable amount of time alone working on plans. But God will use it all to prepare you and give you courage and resilience if you refuse to abandon His mission for your life. After Moses led the Israelites out of Egypt, they wandered for forty years in a state of idolatry and complaining before the promised land was possessed. During that time, God never gave up on them. He provided despite their bad attitude and disobedience; He remained faithful to His promises, but when the time to transition into maturity came, God started to demand more responsibility from them, and the manna ceased. God has a habit of speaking and then suddenly withholding His voice to allow us to walk through this process. Hebrews 5:14 (KJV) says, "But strong meat belongeth to them that are of full age, even those who by reason of use have their senses exercised to discern both good and evil." What you do during those silent times is the same thing you do when taking any test; focus on the task and answer the questions as best as you can. If you were paying attention and retained the information studied, coming up with the answers shouldn't be a problem, right? Well, like the Israelites, sometimes our minds forget or become distracted, which means we will have to take a little longer on the path.

God's plan was to position me in the places where I was needed, and even though obstacles distracted me along the way, His silence helped me retain what I needed to get me to my future assignments eventually. In college, I heard His still, small voice constantly, but the noise of partying, assignments, and independence made it very difficult for me to listen. When I moved back home and eventually reached the end of myself, I surrendered to doing things God's way. I became aware of this conditioning, but the artificial parts of my personality had a hard time leaving. In His getting-ready plan, there is no demand for perfection; the hardest part of the process is letting go of fear and guilt from our past. God's mercy is always available to us. In the book of Genesis 45:8 (NKJV), Joseph had to extend mercy to his fearful and guilt-ridden brothers who sold him into slavery by explaining the truth of God's power over the events of life, "So now it was not you who sent me here, but God; and He has made me a father to Pharaoh, and lord of all his house, and a ruler throughout all the land of Egypt."

I used to have a very hard time responding kindly to the guilt and fear in others. When we cross paths with people who once rebuffed or snubbed us in retrospect, we'll discover how their opinions and actions got us to a better place in life with a greater purpose. Proverbs 29:25 (NKJV) says, "The fear of man brings a snare [trap], But whoever trusts in the LORD shall be safe." The journey to God's safety unfolded gradually as I turned my attention from people's opinions to receiving healing from the poor condition of my heart. Chronic trauma can cause us to lose focus on God guiding our footsteps and place a higher value on what has been done to us, but Joseph didn't surrender to the adverse conditions that got him to a position of greater influence.

During one of my group therapy sessions, my therapist asked me to read a passage out loud, and even though I was hesitant, I did it anyway. The more he insisted that I keep reading, the more frustrated I became until he stopped me, looked me in the eye, and said, "You have a right to say no." After that, I started noticing all the opportunities I ignored to speak up as God placed me in the right environments to practice asserting myself. At my new job, I was surrounded by more seasoned professionals and a diverse reach of customers, which forced me to develop a thicker skin and drop my passive-aggressive act. Unlike my former job, there was no one holding my hand or cuddling my shyness. The first few years were challenging, but I found my agency quickly as I was faced with the demand to find solutions to problems outside of my control daily; it was what I needed to regain the confidence and emotional maturity required to live a balanced life.

Passivity causes us to lose the courage to say no without explanation when required, limits our ability to walk away from manipulation, and we neglect opportunities to stand up for ourselves. My real voice was buried under accomplishments, behind aggressive personalities and opportunities I shied away from but was qualified to handle, but that career shift ended my excuses. Once the enemy understands what fears drive you, his goal is to use it to destroy whatever dream God placed in your heart, but God's sovereignty is beyond reproach; He can use the weaknesses the enemy exploits for your good. Besides learning the skill of avoidance in social isolation, I developed the skill of reasoning, which strengthened my ability at meditation and observation; it helped me narrow in on facts, simplify steps to a solution, and communicate more clearly. I also became more sensitive to spiritual revelations specific to God's personal instruction for my life during the silent period of my life, which He used for a few heroic acts of faith in my future. The environment God chose gave me space to grow, the group dynamic required a more autonomous mindset as my teammates worked in other countries, and I obtained more advanced privileges of managing my own time.

A "quiet period" is a set time when a company cannot release nonpublic information. The goal is to reduce the risk of fraud, such as insider trading.[2]

Transitions usually require a return to obscurity where you talk less and listen more, allowing God to lead you moment by moment. From an idealistic perspective, the wheel in the middle of a wheel described in Ezekiel 1:16–18, which is a function of the multidirectional

2 Bohn, Aimee. "Quiet Period: A Guide for Ipos and Public Companies." Investment U, December 1, 2021. https://investmentu.com/quiet-period-ipo/.

quality of God's nature, can be viewed as Him working in tantum with our obedience and free will to get us to specific destinations. The freedom I discovered when I surrendered my independence to God to embrace His way of doing things helped me manage the quiet periods in my life more delicately. I spent years listening to gifted writers, journaling my thoughts, and reading about whatever I needed to learn at each stage of my journey. Uncovering your purpose in Christ is a daily experience of giving God control of your steps to place you in rooms with people who push you closer to the center of His will for your life, and many of them will not be nice.

As I am writing this, I have no idea how I will finish. This is the first time I am attempting to write a book, and it was trauma recovery that pushed me here. One day, I just sat in front of the computer and started writing after years of saying I will author and publish books someday. Years prior, I didn't have the right language or motivations. My positive reinforcements were other people creating impactful things out of the limitations of the pandemic, and the negative reinforcement was my need to expose the losses I incurred from years of passivity. In the process, I learned how to organize my thoughts logically and creatively as I started using my personal laptop less for social media and more for writing and recording my voice. Afterward, I built up confidence and asked God to help me get published; then, the finances came with His "don't rush" deadline.

That place of surrender and quiet is a time forced to get busy extracting information, acquiring resources, learning from experts, and, more importantly, listening for God's voice. Society has a mold waiting for anyone who dares to step outside of anonymity to do great things, and the quiet time is when character and work ethic are developed; it gives us a deeper appreciation for the processes, being hidden for purpose and an appointed time. I like to think of myself as a natural introvert and a supernatural extrovert. I am not ashamed to admit that I am not excited about the attention that comes with the things God assigns to me sometimes, but an understanding of God's love for me is establishing a firm foundation within my heart to face applause and criticism. The third chapter of Zephaniah explains how God's love takes us on a personal voyage of repair and restoration during times of surrender when we are ready to declare victory over the enemy of our identity. The Lord your God in your midst, the Mighty One, will save; He will rejoice over you with gladness, He will quiet you with His love, He will rejoice over you with singing.

The admiration we seek so desperately when building our identity with external accomplishments must be replaced with the internal love found in a relationship with Christ as we embrace His perfect grace toward us. The false image, fake smiles, and attention seeking we use to impress people lose their appeal when we find God in the quietness of embracing our true self and as we acquire comfort from being seen by Him. To the wife who lost the attention of her husband but still showers him with love, to the man who continues to work overtime to provide for a family that hardly says thank you, to the mom who sacrifices her desires consistently so her children can succeed, or the preacher that spent hours preparing a sermon to a sometimes ungrateful congregation, let God's love quiet you as you listen for His voice rejoicing over you as you fight through your performance. God wants us to reach a place of contentment in Him where time with Him is inclusive of our jobs, family, and recreation; He wants to provide a consistent flow of energy through His validation to make life easier for us. Excluding Him results in lost time and wasted energy as our obligations increase; therefore, be intentional about inviting Him into your daily moments and allow quiet time to become the norm, not just a special occasion. I imagine that feeling of emptiness we get when house guests leave is how God feels when we let Him into intimate spaces of our lives occasionally; He wants a permanent invitation.

The growing pains of life are never fun. They hurt and sometimes take longer than expected. I used to enjoy toning out my struggles with any amount of entertainment, shopping, and good conversations, but making some room for God to come along not only makes the time more enjoyable but more efficient. I like asking His opinion on finding a good parking space, helping me remember what I didn't have on a list; I even ask Him to show me Himself in movies I watch. Worship is not limited to lifting our hands to Him during a song or sermon. When you constantly thank Him for His goodness through daily provisions, you'll discover Him wanting to bless you more and more in real time.

When I started experiencing God in this way, it changed the way I saw Him; He's no longer a distant entity with limited access but an up-close and personal God that is always present. Instead of waiting to go a weeklong fast or praying for hours to get God to move, just make Him your everyday friend and watch Him answer prayers immediately as you include Him in every area of your life. The Bible describes this as delighting yourself in the Lord and Him giving you the desires of your heart (Psalms 37:4). It is you seeking first the kingdom of God and His righteousness, then having Him add all these things to you (Matthew 6:33). It is you doing your part and Him answering with what He promised based on His Word. As His goodness rubs off on you, you'll find yourself wanting to make the hard but better choices to show mercy and deny the desires that cause you to abort His plans for your future.

"Let us therefore come boldly unto the throne of grace, that we may obtain mercy, and find grace to help in time of need" (Hebrews 4:16, KJV).

In my daily pursuits of asking God for help, without realizing it, I was becoming more dependent on His courage to live my life boldly. In my career, I lived by the code of conduct to respect the chain of command, but sometimes you can lose momentum asking the person closest to the one in charge, having to wait patiently for them to get back to you; if you're too patient, they can string you along until you give up. One day, I used the chain of command to avoid a strong personality I knew had the answers to a problem; even with limited time, I let intimidation get the best of me, deciding to take a more passive approach. Two weeks later, after the assistant came back with a no, I decided to ask directly and unexpectedly got not only one but two options to resolve the problem but, in the meantime, lost a lot of money and time.

Fear of man and rejection is the kryptonite to faith and progress; if these two forms of intimidation have held you back as they did for me, this is a friendly reminder to stop wasting your time and the time of those God called you to serve. Because of the death and resurrection of Jesus, there is no longer a physical mediator standing between God and us; we have direct access to His presence to ask boldly. If life is pushing you around and you don't have the energy to fight back, know that there is fullness of joy in God's presence waiting for you. I didn't know how to ask for mercy during that dark period of my life, but the Holy Spirit did. I wish I could tell you this is where the story of trauma ended, but our world is not designed that way, which is why you must go beyond interest and make a commitment to follow Christ if you haven't yet. Fear will always be with us, but having God gives us the advantage in the fight to maintain peace, safety, and sanity throughout life. I stand on the belief that there are only two answers: yes or no. When we don't ask, our needs will remain unmet, and all that is left is desire.

Before I quit my job, I had a nagging desire to pursue something more challenging, but I assumed I could never find better benefits or fulfillment elsewhere, so I just settled. But through adversity, I learned to ask and keep asking in faith, not doubting, believing that God would continue doing impossible things if I remained open to receiving from Him.

CHAPTER 4

Course Correction: "Seen and Heard"

"But we all, with unveiled face, beholding as in a mirror the glory of the Lord, are being transformed into the same image from glory to glory, just as by the Spirit of the Lord."

2 Corinthians 3:18, NKJV

Webster defines unveiled as open or revealed; the word is further explained as showing or announcing publicly for the first time. When God said let us make mankind in our image, according to our likeness physically, He matched the human identity from the smallest to largest parts with His nature; His triune essence is replicated in our brain, nervous system, and cells, which are all divided into three parts. When we receive Christ into our hearts, the unveiling of our true nature, unlike the past event of physical birth, is a progressive experience that uncovers our identity in Christ beneath all the insecurities, flaws, and lies within our thinking. These defects cause confusion and alterations in the way we see ourselves. If we don't renew our minds with the Word of God and rely on His Spirit daily, it is hard to completely detach from the negative effects of our past. When I felt fully seen (unveiled) in the sight of God, habits that caused me to embrace victimhood lost their grip on my lifestyle and allowed me to regain control of my life; now, when I look in the mirror of His word, the victim does not appear anymore. This is the word that came to Jeremiah from the Lord,

> "Go down to the potter's house, and there I will give you my message." So I went down to the potter's house, and I saw him working at the wheel. But the pot he was shaping from the clay was marred in his hands; so the potter formed it into another pot, shaping it as seemed best to him.
>
> Jeremiah 18:2–4 (NIV)

The quality of my life seemed ruined by all the mistakes I made, and I didn't understand how God could use my failures to bring good things into my life, but He did. God showed Jeremiah how our response to His guidance can limit or expand His use of our lives. When I think about the stories that shaped my life, those that limited my potential were always predicated on how I felt about myself; when I thought I wasn't good enough, I showed up unprepared, but when I acquired more confidence from God, I did my research and showed up organized nothing could stop me.

The story of Hagar is a perfect depiction of how the unveiling experience ignites the healing of our identity with God's validation. Genesis 16:13 (NLT), "Thereafter, Hagar used another name to refer to the LORD, who had spoken to her. She said, 'You are the God who sees me.' She also said, 'Have I truly seen the One who sees me?'" Hagar, a slave to Sarah, was caught in an unfair situation; she was given to Abraham, Sarah's husband, to conceive a child and then later exiled. When given access to her master's husband, Hagar became prideful and boastful; slaves were considered property and endured inferior treatment, but Sarah and Abraham's actions gave her a sense of belonging and validation. During her abandonment, she was comforted by the victimhood and self-pity that usually accompany rejection, but when God acknowledged her, the sense of belonging she lost returned and gave her the courage to face shame and dishonor with courage.

Rejection has a crippling effect on the mind. As a child, I sometimes found myself overwhelmed with the feeling that I would never fit in until I encountered the love of God; He showed me how my attachment to self-pity was hindering His healing process and kept me stuck in a poor self-image. I had bought into the lie that God made me quiet, shy, and defenseless; therefore, I lived with low self-worth, feeling unqualified for love and joy, even though I looked like I had it all together on the outside. God sent me many great opportunities, but I disqualified myself due to this mindset; if I didn't work for it in some way, I didn't deserve it. If someone did me a favor, I had to pay them back. If it was expensive, I had to earn it. If he was handsome and interested, something was wrong with him. The list of ungracious ways I treated myself was endless before I let God into my thoughts. Sounds familiar? After I began to entertain the thought that maybe I was really qualified, I stopped hiding behind celebrating others more than myself; the thoughts of equality and abundance helped me accept whatever God said I could have without having to earn it. Like Hagar, I simply changed my response when I saw myself through God's eyes. During the publishing process, I consulted with a few people for wisdom; I wasn't questioning God's provision or approval but needed guidance about the process. In my timid mindset, I would have retreated after hearing objections, but my years of handling rejection in the sales environment taught me differently. The fact is every once-unknown-now-successful person had to face the same ambivalence and objections; in God's kingdom, there is enough room for all of us. God is the potter that shapes and molds us into what He sees best; what gives us leverage individually is our openness to learn more about His will and obey His instructions as He guides us through life.

"So then faith comes by hearing, and hearing by the word of God" (Romans 10:17, NKJV).

After I got to a place where my faith was strong enough, I asked God to give me a vision for my life and the confidence to be myself no matter how intimidating life got. When Hagar's need to belong was restored by God's validation of her and her son, she returned to her former position with confidence to withstand the inferior treatment that came along with being a slave. Moreover, God's acceptance also gave her purpose to live beyond difficult circumstances after she was forced to move on. Genesis 21:17–18 (NIV),

> God heard the boy crying, and the angel of God called to Hagar from heaven and said to her, "What is the matter, Hagar? Do not be afraid; God has heard the boy crying as he lies there. Lift the boy up and take him by the hand, for I will make him into a great nation."

Identity and purpose are powerful motivators; they give the human spirit reasons to hold on when feelings of defeat and disappointing thoughts enter the mind;

they give you the right to be wherever you are sent and remain there. I have been in many difficult work environments throughout my career that required a high degree of emotional intelligence; having a working vision for my life helped minimize the negative energy I had to absorb daily. We all have a breaking point, but God knew Hagar could overlook the painful parts of her life if she had a reason to continue serving when the odds were against her. Jesus explains in John 5:41–43 (NKJV),

> I do not receive honor from men. But I know you, that you do not have the love of God in you. I have come in My Father's name, and you do not receive Me; if another comes in his own name, him you will receive.

Jesus understood His assignment was established in His identity and purpose in God, which made His journey to the cross more important than the obstacles He faced getting there.

"Therefore whoever confesses Me before men, him I will also confess before My Father who is in heaven" (Matthew 10:32, NKJV).

Within each generation, there are inventions and trends that help identify people who were born during that time, from baby boomers to Gen Zs. No matter how much we try to recycle cultural norms to tell stories through fashion, music, and movies, their origin can always be traced to a specific era. Our identity is shaped by the culture of our generation and is so personal that we often alienate others during conversations when we start to reminisce on the good ole days and try to defend our experience as "the standard." As time passes, we are forced to adjust due to changes in society's standards and laws, but in God's kingdom, His standards remain the same. Jesus spoke to His generation within the context of their culture but always challenged the motives (reasoning) of their hearts; why are you really doing what you do? How will it affect the future positively or negatively? Jesus' purpose was to always honor God's name no matter where He went. He pointed people to His Father as the origin of His purpose, belonging, and behind everything He did. Knowing the thinking of the people was shaped by the laws of the Old Testament covenant established prior to His coming to the earth, He had to work very hard to shift their focus to honor the humanity of people more than keeping rules and norms. His healing on the Sabbath and associating with the people who were seen as outcasts challenged the standards and norms of His era and removed barriers created by a class system; He came to provide salvation for everyone.

At the height of Jesus' ministry, He reinforced this new way of thinking to reprioritize the fact that true worship belongs to His Father, who cares deeply about the condition of the heart more than appearance and rituals. He set a standard that no man could attain without receiving and relying on His Spirit; it is what gave the apostles, prophets, and disciples the courage to be different and proclaim God's truth at the expense of embarrassment, being misunderstood, and death.

I became a fitness lover in my late teens because I was too shy to compete on any athletic team in high school; although, sometimes, I was assigned to sporting activities, I was never chosen to be a part of any starting lineup. But one day, during a track event, a star athlete needed to rest in between races, and insanely, my name was called to take her place, which I took as God's way of punishing me for being too quiet. As I walked towards that starting line, I was thinking, *This is not going to end well. God, You must intervene, or I'll just have to fake a fall.* Well, He must have heard me because right before the start, the coach pulled me out of the race. I was so relieved to avoid the embarrassment of losing my already shaky social life, and I didn't have any money to run away from home. Winning was never a big deal to me; the introvert in me was always willing to let someone else try because I was afraid of failure and trying new things. Once God changed the condition of my heart to being accepted and approved, I learned to push past those fears throughout my adult life, and failure became my ally. Now that I have survived more awkward situations, a track event today would be more fun than embarrassing; the fear of not being fully accepted is a human condition we all must face. Jesus did not allow it to undermine His purpose, and we can do the same by embracing God's standards to form our motives.

There is freedom in making peace with your limitations. It takes a lot of pressure off you to admit that you're not good at something, knowing then saying I was made to do this instead, and that is good enough; it can help many of us detach from unnecessary stress. We live in a society that places more emphasis on being good at multiple things as we minimize the quality of executing one task at a time. The message of being good enough has become more about building a brand with limitless possibilities. Jesus had to constantly remind His accusers that His identity did not depend on the validation of men, and this message is even more important today as mental disorders and crime rates increase because of greed across the globe. Fortunately, the self-care movement that is echoed today, focusing on mental health and holistic living, challenged our priorities in the wake of the COVID pandemic; people seemingly became more selfless and empathetic as death swept away countless families for two years. We were all guilty of being caught up in the pride of life, achieving and acquiring all we could and taking less and less time for God and family, but the pandemic brought us back to choosing balanced living.

I don't look forward to going on luxurious vacations as much as I did anymore or shopping sprees to reward myself for all the hustle I put into my career, but I intentionally look for ways to invest more of my time, wisdom, and resources in people after seeing the fragility of the human experience over a prolonged period. About two weeks ago, my hope in the ability of humanity to be kind and unselfish was renewed as I was traveling on a flight from Canada with my mom, who has mobility issues. As we boarded our flight, several people in first class offered us their seats in exchange for a coach seat to accommodate her; it was a moment when I saw God at work in the hearts of people who had survived the uncertainty of ever being able to travel onboard an airplane again. If you look closely, you'll see more opportunities to act out Jesus' message of people over rules in real-time; there are many who survived those two years physically but are still recovering mentally. It was the slowdown we all didn't know we needed that became the catalyst for the importance of maintaining better mental health.

Here is a list of things God led me to do after I surrendered self-pity to receive healing from the self-centeredness that caused chronic imbalances in my life:

I Surrounded Myself with Wise Counsel

Timidity and a fear of failure made me wise, in my own opinion. I tried to live life mostly based on my experiences and the way I saw things, which the Bible calls foolish. But when my heart became pliable enough to receive advice, I began to observe, listen, and ask questions of people who had more knowledge about any area where I struggled. Over time, when I noticed the unnecessary mistakes declining as my quality of life improved, I wasn't afraid of failing anymore and, more importantly, refused to continue living at a disadvantage. Humility is God's pathway to gaining clarity, wisdom, and safety.

Proverbs 18:1 (BSB), "He who isolates himself pursues selfish desires; he rebels against all sound judgment."

Proverbs 11:14 (NKJV), "Where there is no counsel, the people fall; But in the multitude of counselors there is safety."

Practice Listening, Writing Things Down, and Speaking Less

My introverted nature makes me skilled at silence and observing, but my assertive side gives me a passion that makes me overly ambitious sometimes. To tame this, I must intentionally slow myself down by tempering my need to talk and allowing others to speak while listening attentively. Every morning after my time with God, I turn on Christian television to get spiritual instructions and inspiration for the day ahead. One hundred percent of the time, the messages align with something I've been praying or reading about. My primary way of learning is auditory and visual, but writing helps refresh my memory and sharpen my listening skills; I still struggle at times, but I am getting better.

Proverbs 17:28 (ESV), "Even a fool who keeps silent is considered wise; when he closes his lips, he is deemed intelligent."

Proverbs 12:15 (ESV), "The way of a fool is right in his own eyes, but a wise man listens to advice."

Face Rejection

As I learn to face my fear of rejection, the Holy Spirit is teaching me how important it is to respect choice and not take being rejected so personally. There are specific people that fit your life and some that don't; no matter how attractive or rational it may seem, there is freedom in accepting "no" with respect and letting go of offense sooner. Rejection is uncomfortable; whether it's for your good or bad, someone will be hurt. Learning how to let my heart feel the loss and not suppress it is a crucial step I had to practice in overcoming the pain of rejection. Something or someone is gone, and to grieve and then move forward is natural. Moreover, when I look at the feeling of rejection as a given to get through a phase, it motivates me to push through objections and relapses persistently. Detaching and resetting after rejection is a process that takes time, effort, and a positive perspective.

First Corinthians 13:4–7 (NIV),

> Love is patient, love is kind. It does not envy, it does not boast, it is not proud. It does not dishonor others, it is not self-seeking, it is not easily angered, it keeps no record of wrongs. Love does not delight in evil but rejoices with the truth. It always protects, always trusts, always hopes, always perseveres.

Learn How to Resolve Conflict without Abandoning Divine Connections

There are some connections you make in life that have a divine purpose; they are called providential relationships and are designed to help sustain you through a phase in life or throughout your entire life. They usually go beyond the superficial; it can be your inner circle made up of a given or chosen family, friendships, or a community that helps you remain accountable for your true self and purpose. And help steer you away from distractions to your destiny. Unfortunately, because they know you so well and adverse circumstances always happen, there will always be conflicts to resolve; our thoughts and experiences evolve out of sequence often. No two people will react the same way to the same problem, which makes understanding and effective communication vital to the longevity of these relationships. For me, the art of allowing the process of conflict to happen uniquely means giving myself and others space instead of evictions when required. Sometimes, a connection may mean distance and openness to reconciliation while resetting boundaries.

Proverbs 27:17 (ESV), “Iron sharpens iron, and one man sharpens another.”

Proverbs 17:17 (KJV), “A friend loveth at all times, and a brother is born for adversity.”

Manage Your Social Energy

God made us for acceptance, to be acknowledged and seen, but if you have a more introverted nature, excessive energy to socialize is non-existent. The extroverted side of my personality makes it easy for me to connect with people from different backgrounds and different personalities, but I constantly pace myself in social settings because the dominant part of my personality requires smaller doses of attention. When I became more self-aware of this, I learned how to be honest about my energy limitations when socializing by intentionally setting aside time to do nothing or disengage after a certain time. Recharging in solitude after spending a long period of time socializing with people is a necessity in the rules of engagement for introverts with extroverted jobs. We navigate life differently, and the sooner I understood this, the more balanced my life became.

Galatians 6:5 (ESV), "For each will have to bear his own load."

Colossians 4:6 (ESV), "Let your speech always be gracious, seasoned with salt, so that you may know how you ought to answer each person."

Acts 17:26 (ESV), "And he made from one man every nation of mankind to live on all the face of the earth, having determined allotted periods and the boundaries of their dwelling place."

Practice Doing Difficult Things

Surviving a crisis and being able to inspire others through it is very empowering. I have learned that going through difficult things makes it easier to push through internal and external obstacles; it makes you resilient and difficult to offend when you work through hard things. You also build character that you could never learn by just watching someone else's experience. Most of the difficult things I have experienced required forgiveness and patience for myself; sharing this testimony is one of the most difficult but therapeutic things I have ever done in my life. The best writing happened as I went through painful physical and emotional circumstances. Facing difficult things helps you pursue and achieve your goals boldly.

Proverbs 24:10 (ESV), "If you faint in the day of adversity, your strength is small."

Hebrews 12:3 (BSB), "Consider Him who endured such hostility from sinners, so that you will not grow weary and lose heart."

Isaiah 50:7 (NLT), "Because the Sovereign LORD helps me, I will not be disgraced. Therefore, I have set my face like a stone, determined to do his will. And I know that I will not be put to shame."

Psychologist Alfred Adler first described the superiority complex in his early 20th-century work. He outlined that the complex is really a defense mechanism for feelings of inadequacy that we all struggle with. In short, people with a superiority complex frequently have boastful attitudes toward people around them. But these are merely a way to cover up feelings of failure or shortcomings.[3]

---

3 Holland, Kimberly. "Superiority Complex: Understanding It, Traits, Treatment and More." Healthline, August 29, 2019. https://www.healthline.com/health/mental-health/superiority-complex.

Having low self-worth can manifest itself from being abandoned and rejected in the formative years of life; some of us develop an exaggerated sense of importance to compensate for the love or attention we didn't get as children well into adulthood. The superior exterior is a mask for internal feelings of inferiority. These weaknesses we hide behind achievements and perfectionism never seem to go away on their own; they require exposure and then confrontation with grace and truth. During my time serving in the evangelism ministry at church, when we walked through less fortunate communities, my heart broke for the physical conditions the people endured daily, but even more so for their spiritual deprivation. As we talked about God, there was a sense of alienation in the eyes of many as they revealed in their stories that they believed God existed but could not put into words any personal reality of His presence being available to them all the time; He was more like an entity than a friend.

In many circles, the Christian experience is still limited to a few hours in church on Sunday or whenever there is a need to pray. The Bible describes God as an interactive, caring Father; His collaborative nature is exemplified by individual believers through our daily interaction, giving, and use of our gifts on His behalf. As we canvassed the neighborhood, there were groups of young children at home, older individuals living alone, and young men roaming the streets who had little to no daily relational experience with God but saw Him as we talked with them, left supplies, and invited them to church. It was rewarding to see souls won for Christ, but I always wondered about those who didn't feel worthy enough for God and where that unrelatable view of Him came from. Does the church really project a superior stance that perpetuates this negative outlook, or was it made up? In the corporate environment, I encountered many well-dressed, educated people who struggled with faith in God and found it hard to confide in Christian co-workers because we acted like we always had it together. Unlike the one-time evangelism visits, we spend more time with them than with our own family. When I started taking time to see people beyond their titles and economic status, I discovered that they didn't want to see my perfection or hear my deep knowledge of the Bible but needed me to relate to their humanity first. I began to question, "Are we treating everyone with equal respect? Does anyone want to confide in us when they are going through a hard time?" These are the basics of brotherly love.

Jesus closed the gap of superior and inferior views that existed between God and humanity when He sacrificed His life for all; those who don't know Him are watching to see if we really know the Christ we endorse. Is His character in us? Do we have the humility and courage to be transparent about our struggles and show evidence of how we are getting to or got to deliverance? Or are we just putting on an act? His fruits are the evidence to our claims; they make us stand out as representatives of Christ and help us live accountable and consistent lives to people who need to know Him personally. I know it sounds like a lot of pressure, but if we start with the basics, we can change the entity many see into the person He is.

"What has been will be again, what has been done will be done again; there is nothing new under the sun" (Ecclesiastes 1:9, NIV).

I used to wonder why Hollywood studios insisted on remaking popular action hero movies as time progressed, not considering the evolution of generations required new depictions of classics to keep the characters' storylines alive. One way we keep the message of Jesus alive is by telling His story with our lives, how He rescued us from destructive habits and lifestyles to a life of freedom. Before I decided to live a life surrendered to God and stop trusting myself so much, I felt very uncomfortable about sharing my struggles and journey to deliverance because I thought my problems were unique. I didn't realize how wrong I was until I couldn't maintain stability in my relationships, much less manage my entire life properly without Him and a community. I think we make a big mistake waiting until we are completely delivered to share our testimony. Even though it feels better to boast about being free, people who still struggle and suffer privately often get lost in the narrative of the perfect ending we often like to portray. When I became more vulnerable, and others shared their struggles, I gained a greater appreciation for the process than the endings.

I remember the first time I fell hard in public in the middle of the day. I was walking through a busy downtown, all dressed up for work; I lost my balance, missed a step, and in seconds, found myself on concrete with most of my belongings scattered in different directions. When I regained consciousness, I had to pick up my shoes and bag that went flying yards away from me; the embarrassment was not as painful as my body staggering back to the office. As I brushed the dirt off my clothes during my commute, I heard people asking me if I was alright, but clearly, I wasn't. When I got back to work and recounted the story to my co-workers, they each told stories about losing their step and falling in public; some recalled tumbling down a flight of stairs. It was hilarious, but the comedic relief I needed to continue working. While we were retelling our experiences, I recognized a common theme: no one person took themselves that seriously; this is what separates people who know they are flawed from unrelatable perfectionists. When we continue to push through adversity by seeing failure and weaknesses as common, empathy closes the gap between the "us and them" thinking. While a fall is a light failure, sharing the more serious and deeper issues we face requires wisdom and keen judgment, which is developed as we spiritually mature with God and others.

Most of the successful people you encounter started somewhere smaller and still struggle with insecurities about being good enough to fulfill their assignments, but they worked with what they had and did not wait for perfection. They fell many times and were probably told to give up; some were probably too shy while others were too expressive, but it's the people who don't cover up their disadvantages and use them proactively that are most relatable. There were probably people who needed to read this years ago; I can simplify my timing to God's sovereignty, but if I am being honest, I could have been obedient sooner if I utilized my flaws instead of concealing them behind superiority. I am not advocating premature or careless disclosure but motivating you to take steps and open your heart again, no matter how cautiously you need to if life has caused you to shut down. Whether through art, theory, or a simple conversation, the purpose of our life is to leave behind a legacy of how to live through the common highs and lows of human experience. There is nothing new under the sun; a generation that has not been born yet will need a prototype of God's grace that will resonate with their personal experiences, and you may be the answer to them being seen and heard.

CHAPTER 5

Mission Control: "A Time to Die"

"There is a time for everything, and a season for every activity under the heavens: a time to be born and a time to die."

Ecclesiastes 3:1–2, NIV

I have always been a planner. I don't like surprises, and even when they happen, I try to adjust very quickly to keep things in balance; if I have a problem and there is a book I can read or a sermon I can listen to, I search for it. The joy of missing out has never been my problem; I like details and find it hard to accept ambiguity as a part of life at times, but there aren't always clear answers to the way life unfolds. At the age of thirty-three, my sister finally received the answer to her prayers to have a baby. She had been married for several years, celebrating close friends expanding their families year after year, when her long-awaited answer to pregnancy came with a cancer diagnosis. Life has a way of forcing you into a corner sometimes, and the only way of escape is fighting your way out; knowing her prognosis would be fatal, she made the difficult decision to honor the life of her son and delay cancer treatment. During the year and a half that followed his delivery, I observed her living out the last part of her life taking trips to his daycare to spend the time she had left in between her chemotherapy and radiation treatments with courage and grace. Her bravery taught me how selfless love truly is.

A few nights before she passed away, as I watched her struggle, I wished I could give her my lungs for just a moment for relief, but then I realized how selfish I was as I saw life disappearing slowly from her eyes; she was exhausted and was ready to go be with the Lord. At that moment, I could have prayed violently and cursed cancer to the pits of hell, declaring she was healed by the stripes of Jesus, but that's not what she wanted. For the first time in my life, I learned how difficult the act of unconditional love is and couldn't see myself anymore, only her pain-free existence. Her last wish was to see the ocean before she passed away, so we arranged a private charter for her to spend what would be her last day looking at the beautiful waters of the Bahamas. Her name was chosen by our mother because it means brave; she was never afraid of a challenge and lived a full life before her death.

There are no surprises to God; He knows the beginning to the end of each of us before we are formed in our mother's womb. He predestined our purpose, and no matter what choices or unfair circumstances take us off His path, His purpose will be fulfilled. Our lives are never wasted, and our choices are lessons for the people watching and for us. My sister decided not to lose twice; her life on Earth would be over, but a new life started through her child. She understood that giving him a chance to live without her was better than not giving him a chance at all. Her bravery helped me understand the meaning of 1 John 3:16 (ESV), "By this we know love, that he laid down his life for us, and we ought to lay down our lives for the brothers." Trouble is guaranteed in this world, but there is always hope and purpose in our pain to help us make choices beyond ourselves.

"Then they willingly received Him into the boat, and immediately the boat was at the land where they were going" (John 6:21, NKJV).

Although Jesus was a man, He had supreme authority over the universe. In this instance, His walking on the water reminded His disciples that His power was not limited to the natural environment and His humanity. The power of the Holy Spirit gives us a supernatural strength to go through very painful circumstances, enabling the natural part of us to accomplish heroics like the difficult choices my sister made; God's grace and courage within our hearts help us make hard choices to forgive, love, or have mercy in the midst the unfair circumstances.

A couple of months ago, I attempted to download an app that was not available in my region of the world and required a virtual private network subscription to gain access. In the spiritual realm, God's Spirit gives us access to things that cannot be seen beyond the natural realm. Before my sister's diagnosis, one night, during prayer, as my mother was thanking God for preserving the lives of her children, the Holy Spirit whispered my sister's name. I believe in healing; I believe in the power of prayer, and I also believe God knows everything, and His knowledge is complete. I prayed and believed with my sister for years, and having to celebrate her pregnancy and then watch her go from cancer diagnosis to death made me very angry and disappointed with God. It was around the same time my health was being attacked, and even though I had access to His supernatural peace to walk through my grief, the anger I felt was so overwhelming that I stopped feeling, and all that was left was silence. I was still aware of God's presence, but I couldn't pray because His answers during that time came with too much difficulty. I wanted to find solace in John 15:20 to snap myself out of the disappointment and despondency, but I really didn't care to. How do we trust God when we don't get what we want? How should we react when He takes instead of giving?

When Jesus said, "If anyone desires to come after Me, let him deny himself, and take up his cross, and follow Me" (Matthew 16:24, NKJV), I didn't realize what denying myself really required until I was forced into uncontrollable situations that ended in tragedy and chronic illness. As a New Testament believer, in theory, I understand that God does not use disease to punish us; all His wrath has been poured out on Jesus, but in practice, the only person I could blame was the one who could heal but didn't. I know His thoughts towards us are peace, not evil; the existence of disease is evil. God is a good God. During my brief departure from the anger and silence that accompanies grief, my mind focused on the good that happened despite my losses. As someone who is still living with an illness and who has witnessed death several times, I allowed myself to process those traumatic events in silence and reflect where I am most comfortable. God does not condemn us for having feelings; He respects our individual limitations.

I used to think of healing as only a destination like living with the absence of disease, but seeing my sister free from the pain and the struggle of cancer, watching her son grow up and be loved by our family, and having access to medical treatment, changed my perspective from complaining to being grateful. God's grace and restoration can be seen in the provisions we take for granted; His mercy is hidden in the processes of surviving. Do I wish my sister was still here, or I didn't have to be on medicine for the rest of my life? Yes, but her healing is complete in heaven, and mine is in process on Earth. Each testimony may seem like God has failed and we had to settle for less, but God didn't walk away when I got silent; He waited until I reached the understanding that death and loss will not disappear from the equation of this life. Our hope is that victory is already ours through redemption in Christ; pain, loss, and suffering will come to a permanent end for all who trust in Him. Whether we choose to show up for the fights in our life complaining or grateful, reject or accept His no to our prayers, God remains the same; He is faithful and the only constant we have in this imperfect world. I am learning to love Him in that same way when I don't get what I want.

I just recently completed a five-day liquid-only fast. There is no other discipline that can bring you to the end of yourself holistically like it; the process is intense but worth the sacrifice. Fasting not only helps to tame your senses and reveal areas of wrong beliefs that challenge your faith but also exposes the motives of the heart. As a person who has faced these and many other traumatic situations, I became a cynic, which did a great deal of damage to my belief system throughout my healing journey. Sometimes, I felt like God had walked me into a luxury car dealership and showed me a new car that had my name on it, but I couldn't see myself driving it; after so much loss, believing for better or best became an uphill battle. Life had taught me to always be on the lookout for the next bad thing based on what I became accustomed to, but over the years, fasting, along with prayer and meditation on His Word, helped me pull down those negative thought patterns. I am a doer and have never been a big fan of waiting, believing I always had to act and vacate when it looked like nothing was happening. Until God started working patience and persistence in me. To help shift me out of cynicism, He engrained a small event in my mind from a flight delay I experienced when I was traveling back home from a business trip to demonstrate how faith works.

As I took my seat on the aircraft, there was a book in the pocket in front of me that someone had left behind; in it was a story about a little girl that was sent to her neighbors' store to collect money owed to her father. The owner kept acting busy, hoping she would give up and leave, but instead, the little girl ignored his tactics, stood up to him, and declared she was not leaving without her father's money. That story stayed with me for years as God progressively asked me to believe in countless illogical opportunities He had assigned to me; it stirred up faith in me to never allow anything God said belonged to me to be taken without a fight. I think it was the same tenacity He gave my sister when cancer asked her to make a choice between her and her child.

Your story may never be as traumatic, but if you're reading this, I believe life has already thrown you a few unfair circumstances that made you feel bullied. There may not be time to think, and a clear solution may not be available in the natural, but that is when all those times you took to pray and meditate on God's Word will give you the courage to make the right choice without considering the risks. If you've gotten used to losing like I had, the walk of faith is more challenging. I have, and still experience, days when cynicism clouds my judgment, but like that little girl, there is unmovable confidence in me to always keep moving forward. The enemy's job is to create doubt and deception as you wait and prepare; his greatest weapon of deception is to help you get around God's timing and move you out of position. His job is to interrogate us until we abort God's plans. John 8:44 (KJV) says, "He [Satan] was a murderer from the beginning, and abode not in the truth, because there is no truth in him. When he speaketh a lie, he speaketh of his own: for he is a liar, and the father of it." God, on the other hand, cannot lie; sin does not exist in Him, and His Word is truth. Keep believing despite the losses, and wait as He restores.

> The LORD will guide you always; he will satisfy your needs in a sun-scorched land and will

> strengthen your frame. You will be like a well-watered garden, like a spring whose waters never fail.
>
> Isaiah 58:11 (NIV)

The Bible depicts powerful examples of how bad choices can delay or destroy destiny through the lives of Samson, David, Solomon, and Abraham. No matter how confident you feel about your life, the decision to ignore your need to depend on God daily affects you and the destiny of others; consequences are never isolated. We all have weaknesses that we choose to give into repetitively, especially if there is medicine we can take to help us manage the adverse results; however, the human body has some universal and individual limitations that cannot be negotiated. As I am writing this, I am recovering from a brutal night of acid reflux because I chose to eat a deep-fried spicy meal that I knew my body would not digest properly. At the time, I convinced myself that all I had to do was take an antacid and drink a lot of water, but instead, I lost hours of sleep, which made it difficult to complete my morning exercise routine, and I had to take additional medicine to resolve the lingering burning sensation in my chest to get through my workday. I didn't have the energy to complete the work I had planned, which set off a ripple effect of cancellations that inconvenienced many. The effects of not having temperance, in this case, were a result of ignoring the root problem of my anxiety issues; the internal issues we delay confronting have an insidious way of destroying our destiny over time.

According to the attachment theory in psychology, humans attach or interact with people who are important to them in four ways: secure, avoidant, anxious, or disorganized. I truly believe taking a holistic approach to self-awareness when we are confronting internal issues is best; the psychological view is important to understand why we repeat behavior that is not advantageous to our life. I struggle with anxiety from time to time, and no amount of relaxation technique or exercise could tame it exclusively; I would jump from one coping habit to the next to keep myself calm, but nothing seemed to stick. Until I learn to be still and have a conversation with God to silence my reasoning. Progressively, God filled the spaces where there were fractures in my heart from years of trying to prove myself. In the heart of everyone is a need to please; if we fail and do not confront those feelings of insecurity the right way, we tend to lean on vices throughout life. Beneath most of our internal anxiety is a need to be attached securely to someone or something stable that we can trust with our weaknesses without shame.

In Genesis 9:18–29, Noah, a man of the soil, began to plant a vineyard. When he drank some of the wine, he got drunk and uncovered himself inside his tent.

Ham, the father of Canaan, saw his father's nakedness and told his two brothers who were outside. Shem and Japheth took the garment and placed it on their shoulders. Then they walked in backward and covered up their father's nakedness. Their faces were turned the other way so they did not see their father's nakedness. Ham was the youngest son of Noah, who was cursed for exposing his father's weakness. We have all been him and the victim of this kind of shame. Shame is a weapon used to make light of weakness and can degrade us into silence. If you take an inventory of the people you can trust with your weaknesses, your family and close friends should be at the top of the list, but that is not always the case. Shem and Japheth's action of honor is still evident in our world today, but the blood sacrifice of Christ is our ultimate covering; when we return to constant dependence on God, salvation gives us power over our greatest weaknesses. Galatians 3:13 (NLT) says, "Christ has rescued us from the curse pronounced by the law." When He was hung on the cross, He took upon Himself the curse for our wrongdoings.

> Then Samson prayed to the LORD, "Sovereign LORD, remember me. Please, God, strengthen me just once more, and let me with one blow get revenge on the Philistines for my two eyes."
>
> Judges 16:28 (NIV)

Getting a second chance to do the right thing is not always granted in relationships, especially when the offense is habitual and negligence is involved. According to Johns Hopkins, chronic anger puts you into a fight-or-flight mode, which results in numerous changes in heart rate, blood pressure, and immune response. Those changes, then, increase the risk of depression, heart disease, and diabetes, among other conditions. Forgiveness, however, calms stress levels, leading to improved health. Outside of small groups, prayer meetings, and Bible study, behind the nice outfits and rehearsed greetings, there is unresolved anger in many hearts from failing; holding on to offense is exhausting, and finding ways to let go permanently is not easy, especially when shame is involved. At this point, Samson decided to stop misappropriating his pain from failure and returned to his dependence on God to use his strength in a more constructive way.

He was born to deliver the Israelites from the Philistines. Before his conception, his mother was barren and was given specific instructions not to cut his hair, which Samson thought was the source of his strength. But it was the Spirit of the Lord that gave him supernatural strength to carry out his assignment. Samson's ego got the best of him, and he made a mistake; like most gifted people, he lost his focus to the external rewards that came with fame and notoriety, but at his weakest, God used the consequences of his ignorance to trap the Philistines and complete his assignment. No matter how badly you mess up, God can use your situation for His glory if He is acknowledged as the source of your strength. Samson finally understood this and got a second chance to use his strength appropriately. Our secure attachment to God frees us from shame. Samson could have played the victim role, but deep down inside, he knew he had distanced himself from God and needed mercy. God gifted him with righteous anger to seek justice, not selfish ambition; it's the same anger Jesus had when He drove the money changers out of the temple and what motivated David to win battles for the Lord. Samson's poor boundaries were his ultimate demise. His ego made him careless about the character of his friends, and his lack of good judgment also made him take his gift for granted.

I am a natural giver who enjoys finding solutions to problems through acts of service, but I had a habit of lowering my boundaries too far, which created many relationship disasters in my life. Giving makes us feel proud and needed, but the feelings of heroism can be seen as validation if you value the applause inappropriately. And if we aren't completely healed from people-pleasing, our altruistic motives can turn into selfish motives. When I became self-aware of this insecurity, God stirred up righteous anger in me to stop wasting resources for false pride and start giving solely to make the lives of others better. You can give yourself a second chance after humiliation by focusing on God's will.

"My sheep hear my voice, and I know them, and they follow me: And I give unto them eternal life; and they shall never perish, neither shall any man pluck them out of my hand" (John 10:27–28, KJV).

As we spend more time with God, His voice becomes clearer and more familiar. In my experience, the inflection is decisive with words unique to my understanding that require little to no explanation; God rarely gives details, especially if He's restoring our trust in Him. This is challenging for a person who loves details. Webster defines "still" as devoid of or abstaining from motion. When I hear God speak, it feels authoritative and caring, which works well for my direct personality. The more we feed our senses with His Word and spend time with Him, the more courage we obtain to obey without question. When we internalize pain, it leads us to deceptive places in our mind and heart.

One day, God showed me how holding on to unresolved pain is like hanging on a ledge with your feet inches from the ground; all it takes is one step to be free, and He knows what the step is for each of us. Our fears often immobilize and isolate us from the right norms, beliefs, boundaries, and relationships that can improve our lifestyle. Fear helps us violate our conscience of truth and live in complacency. When I enlisted help from external sources, God put me in rooms with people who were more successful and progressive, which helped change the image I had inside myself and scared me out of my fear-based thinking. Some people had the same skills, others more and less; all had a jaded past but were doing extraordinary things for God, which destroyed my excuses. Finally, I started seeing myself parking that expensive car God said I could have. Proverbs 26:13 (KJV) says, "The lazy man says, 'There is a lion in the road! A fierce lion is in the streets!'" The truth is excuses are usually established in insecurities we know are lies, but it's never too late to do better.

If you're not well-connected, God can give you better friendships. What I admired the most was how the new people He connected me to ignored and minimized their inadequacies. Hyper-vigilance and the inability to trust are side effects of chronic trauma; it is understandable if you need to take time to rebuild your network, but don't allow failure to prevent you from trying again. After God helped me connect to more positive reinforcing environments, I moved away from disruptive circles quickly to prevent myself from relapsing into the anxious person I was in the past. As I continued the process of internal healing, it was the work He did to improve the relationship I had with myself that helped me remain in these environments; I had gained a greater appreciation for transparency and genuine connections with secure people. I saw this transparency and security played out in the healthy relationships around me growing up; the successful couples instinctively knew when to catch up or slow down when communicating with each other and were more adaptable to change, which helped them remain united.

The truth of who we are takes a lot of digging through layers of lies we accepted as truth for a long time, but God's Spirit in us can heal and restore the quality of our lives and help us navigate change effortlessly. My learning to step away from the people and places that didn't serve the healed me was painful; change is lonely, but not being aligned with the right people is even worse and compromises your growth. It's much easier to go along with God's plan as He orchestrates people in and out of your life; trying to control the process delays your healing. In moving forward, I am most influenced by those who are already where I want to be and pay close attention to the character it took for them to get through setbacks with grace. In 2 Corinthians 6:1–8, Paul proclaimed grace helped him to serve in the good and bad times, doing whatever was required by the power of God; adapting to and deliberate change is necessary as we evolve in our purpose, and the good news is we don't have to do it in our own strength.

> So he went and hired himself out to one of the citizens of that country, who sent him into his fields to feed pigs. And he was longing to be fed with the pods that the pigs ate, and no one gave him anything. But when he came to himself, he said, 'How many of my father's hired servants have more than enough bread, but I perish here with hunger! I will arise and go to my father, and I will say to him, "Father, I have sinned against heaven and before you. I am no longer worthy to be called your son. Treat me as one of your hired servants."' And he arose and came to his father. But while he was still a long way off, his father saw him and felt compassion, and ran and embraced him and kissed him. And the son said to him, 'Father, I have sinned against heaven and before you. I am no longer worthy to be called your son.' But the father said to his servants, 'Bring quickly the best robe, and put it on him, and put a ring on his hand, and shoes on his feet. And bring the fattened calf and kill it, and let us eat and celebrate. For this my son was dead, and is alive again; he was lost, and is found.' And they began to celebrate.
>
> Luke 15:15–24 (ESV)

Life's hard truth is that no one person is responsible for your happiness and contentment. Individually, we are obligated to discover our own worth in God, and He cannot rescue us from whatever darkness we face if we are not willing to do our part. Trusting God with desires that have an appointed time requires patience and, unfortunately, some ignorance about how He'll get you there. The prodigal son, like most of us, moved out of a life stage prematurely to acquire that rush of instant gratification. When we don't want to wait and prepare to be the singer, the writer, the business owner, wife, or husband, we delay God's plans; trying to skip steps and getting to the destination sooner often ends in disaster because we are unprepared for the full weight of the assignment. Doing things God's way is inconvenient.

Today, I didn't attend church as usual because I needed to rest from a challenging work week, so I woke up early to do laundry before watching church online. When I got there, it was crowded, so I had to push past laundry baskets, used dryer sheets on the floor, and people rushing around machines, but I had to get the laundry done even if it meant choosing machines far apart. Without saying a word, intuitively, I began to preach a sermon to myself, recognizing how my need for convenience and instant gratification was working against me; our desires don't like to be inconvenienced, and if they are not tempered, they prevent us from completing phases in our growth on time. At the time, I had stopped my 4 a.m. outdoor workouts, was sleeping in, missing sermons that I listened to as a part of my morning devotion, and regaining weight I had worked so hard to lose the year prior. This poor work ethic was not congruent with the goals I had for myself. Like the prodigal son, I wanted things to happen in my timing, and when they didn't, I went on vacation in my mind. This is not the kind of waiting God has in mind, but restoration of lost time is possible.

Those positive reinforcing friendships God assigned to get me moving again had to give up mediocrity and take some inconvenient paths to reach their goals. If the client wanted to meet at 5 p.m. after a long day at work, yoga class had to be canceled. If a last-minute contract meeting came up as they were getting ready for bed, they got dressed and went despite being exhausted. When the prepared you shows up, mediocrity and excuses will be a thing of the past. The prodigal son discovered that settling for the convenience of having it all now was a waste of time and resources. If the people and places you are surrounded by no longer challenge you to be the version God wants you to be or do not inspire you to do things the right way, choose the inconvenience of realigning yourself with Him. The true test in taking accountability for your happiness is knowing where you fit after you mess up and pursuing it. It takes time to find the right environment that suits the restored you, but the effort is worth it.

"Therefore if any man be in Christ, he is a new creature: old things are passed away; behold, all things are become new" (2 Corinthians 5:17, KJV).

In the new phase of life, God will give you amnesia about certain events and people that will trigger you to revert to the old you. A few days ago, I was trying to recall the name of a guy I dated; it was as if his name had been erased from my mind permanently. Then I remembered a few things I did to detach from him; I erased him from my social media and deleted his number, which I had done in the past, but I never forgot the person's name. When you no longer identify with the person you used to be, the Scripture says old things have passed away; the person I was when I dated him is unrecognizable, and so are the memories. Rebounding is the start of a new beginning; after a life-altering event like a breakup, most women have a habit of changing their appearance; it's necessary for us to seek a therapeutic release, which is usually cosmetic. This physical act of detaching helps us embrace our new way of life, and our new look reminds us of that change. Letting go of the me I used to be meant facing life with no sister nearby to call anymore for advice, a tedious work regimen, and resetting my social circle.

Life was so much easier when I avoided my issues and did not care to fight my way through difficulty, but it was also filled with loneliness and fear-based thinking.

Fortunately, we have a heavenly Father who helps us do the waiting through difficulties we can't on our own; He is always willing to embrace us with compassion when we decide to depend on Him. If you are reading this with the hope of finding a quick solution through a process, effortless change is only possible when journeying with God, finding His forgiveness, and embracing His truth. When you receive God's truth and love, you'll discover the things you depended on to feel worth and wholeness leaving; you become more repentant and realize that change is possible no matter how far you fall. You'll have more courage to deal with losses that are guaranteed in life, take ownership of your feelings, and, more importantly, you'll develop a love for responsibility and hatred for self-pity.

Can you see, taste, and feel that freedom? Can you imagine walking away from the vices you depend on to survive daily and start doing the work of confronting the hurt you refuse to let go of? Make the decision to use your anger for a righteous cause of healing within, become a part of a solution, practice relying on God's strength, and receive His unconditional love. There are people waiting to see your bravery and wisdom, waiting for you to move from a place of despondency to a place of reengaging in life, but you must first do it for yourself. Yesterday is gone, and there is nothing you can do about it, but today, you can choose the lessons and be okay with those unanswered prayers. God's supply is vast; there is no scarcity of goods. He has an abundant life waiting for you as you pick up the pieces. He is patiently waiting. You can walk slowly, and as you allow change to happen imperfectly, His arms remain open wide to receive you with the mistakes, flaws, and disappointment. Whatever you have left is enough; He will multiply it.

> The Lord is not slack concerning his promise, as some men count slackness; but is longsuffering to us-ward, not willing that any should perish, but that all should come to repentance.
>
> 2 Peter 3:9 (KJV)

CHAPTER 6

Gravity: "Answering the Call"

Gravity is the force by which a planet or other body draws objects toward its center. Objects with more mass have more gravity. Gravity also gets weaker with distance. So, the closer objects are to each other, the stronger their gravitational pull is.[4]

When your heart is ready to stop grieving, and your mind receives God's peace, He repositions you to move into rooms with people, opportunities, and plans that were waiting for you. As I drew closer to God throughout life, I found it easy to react to His voice quickly without considering the risks of illogical directives, things that are counterintuitive but end up being a direct answer to prayer.

4 "What Is Gravity?" NASA, December 17, 2020. https://spaceplace.nasa.gov/what-is-gravity/en/.

One summer, when my mom was lying in pain in the emergency room for forty-eight hours, and we were being told there were no hospital beds available for her admission, I got an impression from the Holy Spirit to walk upstairs to a specific ward in the hospital and ask for a bed. Without hesitation, I moved from an active conversation, feeling like I was in space with gravity transporting me to the exact destination I was instructed to go. When I got there, I was told I wasn't allowed access and was breaking protocol, but by the time I got back downstairs, within minutes, my mother was being wheeled upstairs to be placed in a hospital bed. God knew there was a nurse on duty that day who would recognize my mother's name and show her favor, but what if I had ignored Him and given into the fear of being rejected or being put out of the hospital? Would my mother still be alive today? I don't know the answer, but I have developed a keen awareness between a directive and a request from God. Directives don't require explanations, only immediate responses. God has led me to specific people within companies I needed to network with to close sales, asked me to apply for jobs I wasn't fully qualified for and was hired, told me to purchase clothing for trips I didn't know He planned, and asked me to leave great relationships without any explanation. John 10:3 says, "The gatekeeper [Jesus] opens the gate for him, and the sheep listen to his voice.

He calls his own sheep by name and leads them out." This drawing, like gravity, strengthens the closer we get to God.

As an adult, I practice including God in my daily routine, but the habit didn't happen suddenly. As a child, sometimes, I would feel God prompting me to be still and move closer to Him when I moved too far away, like a child reacting to the voice of a mother. I didn't know what to call it at the time, but I learned that the heroic acts of courage I experienced as an adult are referred to as the gift of faith. According to Got Questions,[5] it may be defined as the special gift whereby the Spirit provides Christians with extraordinary confidence in God's promises, power, and presence so they can take heroic stands for the future of God's work in the church. I never thought of myself as a hero, much less a leader. One of my favorite breakfast foods is oatmeal, and I like getting up early and going to bed before 10 p.m. I live for routine. I like structure, and the gift of faith is more inconvenient and uncomfortable; it comes with instability and unpredictability, things I don't like, which I guess is God's way of spicing up my oatmeal routine-loving personality. This is the flight response of faith that is activated quickly to get us in and out of sticky situations, but the fight response of faith is a

5 "What Is the Spiritual Gift of Faith?" GotQuestions.org, n.d. https://www.gotquestions.org/gift-of-faith.html.

bit different. It's when God asks you to do something irrational, the answer is not immediate, and it involves a period of waiting and watching, which cultivates our favorite character trait: patience. Although inconvenient, the type A part of my personality can adapt easily to the flight response. I like getting things done and usually right away, but fighting is something I am still getting used to.

> Then he said, "Take the arrows," and the king took them. Elisha told him, "Strike the ground." He struck it three times and stopped. The man of God was angry with him and said, "You should have struck the ground five or six times; then you would have defeated Aram and completely destroyed it. But now you will defeat it only three times."
>
> 2 Kings 13:18 (NIV)

God uses circumstances to build character in us through the process of answering prayers. The character-building work of faith requires a process that helps to purify our motives and establish our identity for His plans. Just before the death of Elisha, Jehoash, king of Israel, consulted with him for a strategy to win a war, but in haste, the king limited his capacity to win by doing just enough and symbolically striking the ground three times. In haste, we waste a lot of time doing just enough, hoping God will pick up the slack, hoping the problem will just go away with the easiest, less risky response. I am embracing the fact that God is not a fan of shortcuts, especially when He plans to use our lives in a dynamic way. If we ignore His instructions, He takes us the long, hard way through slower timing and processes to make sure the lesson sticks. And He doesn't do this to be cruel; just look at it as His version of quality-driven management.

I had spent a few years ignoring my doctor's advice to have surgery, and just as the world was about to go into a tailspin from the Corona crisis, so was my life; I thought I was done with pain and grief, but my body still needed some attention. Like a computer operating on low battery power, the body gives us warnings when it's time to stop, adjust, rest, and recharge, and if those messages are ignored, God designed it with an internal shutdown switch to take the rest for us. In the winter of 2019, just before the pandemic, I started a thirty-day non-stop exercise program to lose twenty pounds and escape some unresolved emotional issues I didn't care to confront. The combination of dieting and a constant adrenaline rush from working out daily gave me a feeling of contentment that I thought would help me manage my life long-term. Well, thirty days turned into 200 days of non-stop exercise. I kept telling myself it was okay despite chronic joint and muscle pain from inadequate rest, sleep disturbances, and chronic anxiety until I found myself on a psychiatrist's couch crying uncontrollably. He told me what I already knew deep down inside: I was suffering from the effects of prolonged grieving, and the organic problems I suffered made it worse.

After being referred to my primary care physician, I got blood results filled with red flags, resulting in four rounds of iron infusions and surgery immediately after. At the height of the pandemic, I found myself in a medical crisis, entering my first-ever surgical procedure with no visitors allowed, surrounded by COVID patients. After surgery, I almost bled to death in recovery, and a few days after leaving the hospital, I developed near-fatal complications. After failing to reach my family and friends with no time to spare, I crawled to the car in intense pain and drove myself to the doctor's office nearby, who called an ambulance to take me to the emergency room. It all unfolded like a tsunami. I couldn't think about anything else but my faith in God as I spent three months in and out of medical facilities, running out of veins to puncture.

When it was all over, and the medicines wore off, my mental recovery began. I developed post-traumatic episodes that overwhelmed me daily, and I spent months crying myself to sleep every night; it was the darkest emotional pain I had ever experienced, but I insanely asked God to let me go through it. Before this crisis, escape was my way of dealing with internal pain, and I had finally reached a point of no return; it was time for me to stop taking shortcuts and allow myself to feel the pain, face it, and survive to help someone else. During that time, God sent me people throughout the journey to help me process and embrace a new perspective on life. I got back in therapy and stayed there. I gave myself permission to be imperfect and weak again, allowing myself to revisit shame and poor judgment from the past. I started listening to my body when it asked me to stop, rest, be quiet, and slow down; I gave up trying to live up to unrealistic expectations. As I prayed for God's help minute by minute, I saw His answers immediately. I was losing the entitled, self-driven, prideful parts of me again and started experiencing God's grace with more clarity. Only this time, God was doing more of the talking as stillness took over, and the Holy Spirit activated confidence and courage within me to embrace self-awareness as a new way of navigating life with balance.

When we lose someone or something, the love in our hearts does not leave; it may be buried under anger or pain, but it remains. Forgiveness is one of the bravest acts of mercy in life you can give yourself and the most gracious thing we can do for the heart. I never knew what true love was for myself until my life was threatened so intensely. I thought I had already learned my lesson but needed a few retakes.

Being the strong one all the time is an exhausting way to live. I spent a lot of time filling up my days with work to numb the internal pain of loss and insecurities that made me feel misunderstood all my life, and dealing with my childhood wounds was a major part of finding the solution. The living sacrifice spoken of in Romans 12:1 is a new way of life for me. I have seen God provide for me in miraculous ways when all the energy I had was disappearing. When I was at my worst, He never made me feel unworthy or judged for not taking better care of myself sooner; He just kept sending me resources. Who could ask for a better friend? One that can handle all parts of you, specifically the timid you that tries to take the easier route until all else fails. He sticks around and helps us get through the bad choices, which was the best lesson of all.

It's the last month of 2022, the year the world recovered from the COVID pandemic, I have completed over a year of therapy to help with trauma recovery, and I am almost finished writing my first book. To help restore stability to my emotions, my therapist suggested I start a feelings journal and practice letting go. I use this journal to confront any difficult feelings that made me hypervigilant in real time, slow down, and get better sleep. With no judgment, I started to accept my feelings as a natural part of myself that must be expressed within reason. Surprisingly, I discovered psychology and science are right. As I allowed myself to acknowledge my feelings without shame, it became less difficult to deal with reality. I stopped isolating things to extremes and making my issues the whole truth but more so a part of a truth; it was me letting go of perfectionism, and it felt like a fog was lifted from my thinking. In biblical terms, I was taking thoughts captive that contaminated my thinking in exchange for God's truth.

Captive, as defined in Strong's concordance, is to subjugate, to bring under control. In my habitual worried state, I was always in a hurry to find an easier way out of problems to avoid the fear of abandonment; for example, my dog's cancer prognosis. Fear of abandonment told me, "Don't put her to sleep and wait until she gets better," knowing her illness was terminal, my emotions would not allow me to consider her leaving as no more suffering from pain; I just wanted to run from the feeling of living without a pet that I had become securely attached to for fourteen years. She was still mobile, had a good appetite, and was happy, and that's how I wanted it to remain. Choosing to fight the inevitable, I lost sleep and thousands of dollars for months just to avoid a feeling. I couldn't accept cancer as a part of her truth and make peace with all the good times, so I prolonged her suffering without thinking I could acquire another dog in a healthier state. My spiritually atoned side was only able to grasp this after I allowed myself to confront the anxiety and fear by journaling and God's motivation through future adversity that left me no choice.

There is a scene in the movie *Gravity* when two astronauts got caught in a storm and were faced with a decision that left both lives hanging in the balance; one person could survive if the other let go and died. Knowing the weight distribution was too much for the rope, the heavier astronaut cut himself loose after the lighter astronaut refused to let him go. In the book *The Body Keeps Score*, the author describes when our safety is being threatened by difficult changes, the mind will try its best to help us get back to the safety we are used to as quickly as possible, even if that safety is disruptive. I eventually passed the test of letting go of an unhealthy dog, but it was God who helped cut the rope.

"A time to get, and a time to lose; a time to keep, and a time to cast away" (Ecclesiastes 3:6, KJV).

It's 4 a.m. I am dressed in my workout clothes, sitting on my bed with a Bible in my lap in tears. As I sat there contemplating whether I had the strength in me to get back into my old workout routine, I thought about the effort it took to go outside every morning at 5 a.m., but what made me want to give up the most wasn't the activity but the story of trauma I told myself when I couldn't stop exercising. My body had not caught up to what my brain had already resolved; I wasn't the same and was afraid I would trigger myself into that self-destructive person again by revisiting the scene of the crime. For months, I told myself, "One day, I'll get up religiously every morning and do my outdoor routine," but mentally, I just didn't have it in me anymore. In the days ahead, I noticed there were people, things, mindsets, and habits all around me that no longer matched my mental shift, but I wasn't paying attention. I didn't know allowing myself to confront my feelings would help me change physically, but it did; trauma never leaves you the same. As I embraced the recommendations from my therapy sessions, along with doing work daily on my spiritual growth, God was slowly healing my mind and body as I learned to control my emotions. I had to learn the art of letting go of who I used to be. The new me didn't need a daily high-intensity workout anymore to survive. The older and wiser we get, the more out of love we become with hurry, and I didn't realize it was time to slow down. There is less and less energy for relentless proving as you get older; you don't feel like you must earn everything the hard way, and best of all, you stop trying to force your own way through life.

This is how we mature in the waiting process. The patience side of faith means handling the controllable (my part) and leaving the uncontrollable alone (God's part), while God is handling the things outside of our control: the when and how. We work with the Holy Spirit on the what, who, and where. What we learn in waiting is how to accommodate the new, what we believe and say about ourselves now at that stage without thinking about the next, living more in the present, and our desires are more aligned with God's will. When we stop fighting with God, everything around us may feel like a loss and tells us to give up, but His strength helps us move forward. You become more submissive, and you let go, slow down, stand still, or do whatever it takes to finish your part in life. In John Mark Comer's book, *The Ruthless Elimination of Hurry*, he mentions how hurry is from the devil and slow is from Jesus. As I reflect on the times I assumed and then reacted in haste, my motive was always to jump ahead of God like I could beat Him in a race. In the story of the centurion, patience is demonstrated in the confidence placed in Jesus' authority to heal through a spoken word. There was no need to rush Jesus to the location of his sick relative; he understood His power transcends space and time. The spoken word of God is the seed that grows without us seeing the full process; when we wait on the Lord with courage, it gives us faith that the answer is guaranteed. The fear-based reality I once called safety has been cast away, and the seeds of faith God planted as I was doing my part to live better is my new safety. There is no longer a need to run.

> For by grace you have been saved through faith, and that not of yourselves; it is the gift of God, not of works, lest anyone should boast. For we are His workmanship, created in Christ Jesus for good works, which God prepared beforehand that we should walk in them.
>
> Ephesians 2:8–10 (NKJV)

Along with the gift of faith comes a gift of knowledge and wisdom about a situation or person revealed to you by the Holy Spirit. Because these gifts operate together strongly in some people, the expectation that God's answer will come without questioning when or how becomes a lifestyle. Ask any believer with these gifts how they hear from God, and most will describe His voice as being so distinct that it's very hard to confuse it with something else, whether in a crowded room or in a deep sleep. Our answer to prayer does not always show up how we imagine. Man's free will causes delays, rejection, and confusion, but when God speaks to an obedient heart, nothing will separate you from what He has assigned to you in life, no matter how complex the circumstances appear.

We are always waiting for prayers to be answered. What I enjoy the most about the journey to answered prayers is the time spent learning, and if you are teachable, God multiplies His wisdom to you. After my sister's death, God asked me to switch careers and leave a church I had been attending for ten years. At first, I didn't listen; my feelings told me it was the enemy, but I knew it was God. However, instead of obeying, I just kept going and ignored Him until He made it physically painful for me to exist in both organizations. I was comfortable but not growing, and God understood that. For the next year, I spent Sunday after Sunday going from church to church; I visited every denomination that professed Christ. God's purpose was to use the journey as another character-building exercise to get me out of a rigid church-dependent mindset. When you remain open to God's guidance, there are a few things you will get used to: first is being uncomfortable, second is difficulty, and third is saying yes to uncertainty. To humor me, He never let me get comfortable at any church; it was like going on bad dates Sunday after Sunday. Nothing made me want to settle. Every time I got tired and wanted to give up, He sent me an encouraging word that kept me focused on the goal of finding a church. I just couldn't understand why He couldn't tell me exactly where, but

He had to get me comfortable with being uncomfortable for a while, I guess.

One day, I decided to take a break, which turned into a month. I was on my way to shower after working out and had a thought. With all the years I attended church, I knew about God, but suddenly, I recognized a strong desire to know Him personally. Then I came across this man sitting down, teaching about how to experience God through His Word in the plainest way I had ever heard. There weren't any theatrics or gimmicks, and surprisingly, I was fully engaged as he spoke about a side of God I never knew. He was describing a God I didn't have to perform for, that does not condemn me; it was the gracious God I couldn't see being explained in the simplest form. The God he was explaining was safe and kind, He wasn't holding grudges and was waiting for me to receive His goodness. That was when I realized how ignorant I was and how overly dependent I became on church attendance. Sunday after Sunday, I used my finances as a seed for answered prayers to manage my life but neglected my responsibility to know God through His Word. Gifts, like every good thing in life, must be nurtured and preserved; it was time for me to see life through grace and not by works alone.

During my time in the pharmaceutical industry, I could always tell which doctor was most invested in the practice of medicine; he or she attended medical conferences regularly, they were the first to be recommended by their colleagues, and even though they stayed booked and busy, learning about new breakthroughs in medicine was prescheduled throughout the year. So, I started the habit of prescheduling my time with God, and before I knew it, every morning turned into every other moment throughout the day. I did find a church eventually and switched industries in my career, but the main lesson I learned along the way is to never limit God and always remain adaptable to His guidance. Your choices will be criticized, and you may even be called unstable and delusional for a while, but ultimately, your answer to His specific plans for your life is the best decision.

> So it was, from the time that he had made him overseer of his house and all that he had, that the LORD blessed the Egyptian's house for Joseph's sake; and the blessing of the LORD was on all that he had in the house and in the field. Thus he left all that he had in Joseph's hand, and he did not know what he had except for the bread which he ate.
>
> Genesis 39:5–6 (NKJV)

God's way of refining our skills requires time and a teachable posture; being so used to doing things my way, I had to sacrifice a lot of my ego, rigid scheduling, and impatience to catch up on getting things done the long and hard way. Joseph's humble attitude and teachable nature gave him favor with people, specifically those who held leadership positions during his transitions. Like most independent-driven people, I viewed submission as control, but after I accepted the lessons life kept trying to teach me, I started working through circumstances diligently instead of running away from opportunities for growth. In 1 Samuel 3:9, Samuel was not familiar with the voice of God because He had not spoken to him directly before, he was young, and his mentor Eli had to guide him, but the gift of the Holy Spirit gave us direct access to God with the new covenant made with man through the sacrifice of Jesus. First Corinthians 12:7–11 (NKJV) says,

> The manifestation of the Spirit is given to each one for the profit of all: for to one is given the word of wisdom through the Spirit, to another the word of knowledge through the same Spirit, to another faith by the same Spirit, to another gifts of healings by the same Spirit, to another the working of miracles, to another prophecy, to another discerning of spirits, to another different kinds of tongues, to another the interpretation of tongues. But one and the same Spirit works all these things, distributing to each one individually as He wills.

Having a naturally quiet disposition, it's very easy for me to be alone for long periods of time, but God also needed me to learn how to master my extrovert skills for where He was taking me. Despite being from a large family, I don't get an energy kick from being around a lot of people, which is why I still don't understand why God chose me for the gifts He gave me. He uses each of us uniquely and gives us the patience required to develop the skills He has given, no matter what dominant personality trait we possess, but without submission to others and His Spirit, the learning curve takes longer.

I must admit the extrovert side of me is fun. I like talking to people and learning how they experience the world to challenge my perspective about life; God knits us together perfectly and knows what environments are needed to cultivate our strengths and weaknesses, so we can trust any alterations He makes along the way. Trust is what submission is at the core. As I healed from hypervigilance, I endured more tests in trusting my superiors at work, church, and in my personal life to make better decisions. Like Eli, these people have mentorship qualities with more expansive wisdom to assist with problem-solving. During the times my ego challenged me, I continued to rely on God and my superiors to think more logically when trying to resolve issues in my life. If you don't know what gift or gifts you operate in strongly, take some time to reflect on the things you love doing the most and challenge you, then include people you can trust to see things from a different point of view that will expand your thinking. This will require you to move closer to others and give up some of the time you enjoy spending alone. Sorry but not sorry, my fellow introverts. And the greatest fear I had in doing this was losing autonomy.

My mother always had a love for plants, which rubbed off on me later in life. As I was learning more about the nature of different types of plants, the Holy Spirit revealed to me a key to maintaining my true self as God placed me in different environments. There are some plants that can survive indoors or outdoors, can adapt to varying climates, do not need to be groomed regularly, and can be watered sparingly; these kinds of plants are low maintenance. While there are others that like moderate sunlight, need to be groomed regularly, and frequently watered to thrive, I am a lot like the first examples; I don't like being handled or cuddled too much. If you give me an instruction, then leave me alone; I will find a way to get the job done. I am also always ready to adjust to different environments to get along with others, a trait I picked up from being raised in a large family. When you accept the thing or things you have a natural affinity for, the Holy Spirit can guide you on how to use them in numerous ways to glorify God without losing yourself. If trauma has exhausted you and shut down parts of your ability to function wholly, God has an answer for it; full acceptance comes as you confront your greatest fears and struggles to embrace the strong and weak sides of yourself. Being misunderstood is painful when it comes from others but even more damaging when you don't understand yourself.

A few nights ago, I had a dream about owning a small but highly valued artifact that a man asked to purchase. He said he had been looking for one like it for a very long time and would pay anything for it. But all I saw was a small box. I thought, What's the big deal? So, instead, I gave it to him for nothing. When I awoke, the Holy Spirit revealed how I was perceiving my worth as less than what it is because of my weaknesses and overlooked the small things He had appreciated over time in my life. Like young Samuel, I needed to become more in tune with God's voice that says I am worthy and can be confident that He gave me the skills to do whatever He asks. When He positions you in environments that require your gifts, it's His voice you should answer, no matter who or what else calls you. The story of the tenacious little girl waiting for her father's money is still helping me push through life, and whenever I lose esteem, God reminds me of her.

> Peace I leave with you, My peace I give to you; not as the world gives do I give to you. Let not your heart be troubled, neither let it be afraid. You have heard Me say to you, 'I am going away and coming back to you.' If you loved Me, you would rejoice because I said, 'I am going to the Father,' for My Father is greater than I.
>
> John 14:27–28 (NKJV)

I had read that scripture many times, but this time, I found the key that unlocked the door of safety I needed after the smoke cleared from my various crises. Jesus reassured us with the language of security that He was going away but coming back, and He didn't leave us empty-handed; He left the Holy Spirit to comfort and guide us in all truth. These words should heal the hearts of many people who were abandoned, rejected, and forgotten but became codependent on people, habits, and things to cope with life. The internal lasting safety you need is always present. He gives supernatural peace that people and things can't. We all, by nature, are imperfect and self-serving, which is opposite to the nature of the Holy Spirit; He is always ready to serve. The he or she that you once needed may never be able to make up for the hurt you endured, but God will restore safety by leading you to people and resources that can help you feel safe again. He is standing in place with the child inside of you who still feels abandoned and remembers the person who walked away and never came back. No matter how much you cling to the ideal person you created in your mind to deal with the trauma he or she caused, you can only recover what you lost by being the caretaker of your heart in the present. God can help you be what they couldn't be; He can help you start over and be the parent that does show up to games and has the hard conversations. And the sooner you challenge those insecurities, the easier it will be to manage life without ideals. To survive trauma, I learn to walk through the dark tunnel of grief to get to the other side of peace, where I embrace the reality of the here and now; it's painful and scary, but I continue to walk until I see the light. God is there to help you uncover each fear at a time with deep revelations that will sustain you; He's always ready to help you take the journey.

We utilize our gifts daily in our vocation, hobbies, and interaction with the world. It is often said that our gift is something we are passionate about and do with ease. As a sales executive, I have used the gift of faith and wisdom to convince companies to utilize a service or product in long-term business commitments for years. And the skill of humility that comes along with these gifts strengthens my credibility as I work closely with teams to get things done. For instance, when a customer decides to walk away, it's my job to work with others to recover the relationship, improve service, and remain open-minded and reachable. Maintaining connections that ended can also lead to new relationships. I have had several referrals from former clients that turned into long-term business connections. Outside of developing the skill to promote quality products or services, I constantly work on my ability to empathize, trust, and forgive to improve my networking skills, and most of it comes from the self-awareness work mentioned earlier.

Last weekend, I decided to watch a movie that got a lot of buzz because of the popular Hollywood studio that produced it, but there was just one problem: the main character, although gifted, had a bad offscreen reputation with the law, which along with a poor storyline, adversely affected the movie's ticket sales. As much as we like to pretend our personal choices don't have that much influence on our careers, they do; having a poor personal reputation can contaminate and eventually ruin your professional life. Bad character traits don't just surface overnight; we reinforce them daily in small acts of dishonesty. Our good character traits give us more favor with others, but God tends to use us with a mixture as we become better people. As I watched the movie and prayed for the main character personally, it reminded me of God's heart toward anyone who is living without Him. He is not willing for anyone to perish, and redemption is for everyone. Sadly,

I have met many people who are blessed with gifts and talents but lack the character to maintain long-term success because the message of a condemning God still clouds their view of Him. We celebrate their ability and physical appearance and place them on pedestals but forget their humanity, thinking their fame and money are enough. But God is using their gifts to reach the people they influence in ways we can't see, and most of them cater to an audience we'll never reach. We can have all the skills, Bible knowledge, and charisma required to be successful, but if we don't take time to sort out our heart issues and, in turn, pray for those who do not know God personally, are we really seekers of His will?

"But I have prayed for you, that your faith should not fail; and when you have returned to Me, strengthen your brethren" (Luke 22:32, NKJV).

We feel like a failure when we do things that are hard to forgive. Peter had denied Jesus several times and, in his repentance, needed forgiveness instead of retribution: punishment inflicted on someone as vengeance for a wrong or criminal act. If you grew up in an environment filled with a lot of rules and conditional acceptance, it is hard to forgive. Jesus encouraged Peter to strengthen his brothers who, in their own human weakness, are subject to failing; learning how not to punish people who hurt or disappoint us with judgment or contempt takes supernatural help. When we pray for forgiveness to enter our hearts and bitterness to leave, we should pray the same for others. The Bible says the opportunity to be offended will increase. As stated in 2 Timothy 3, unforgiveness is listed as one of many evil traits that people will possess as the return of Christ approaches. Having a grateful attitude and positive outlook about the forgiveness offered in our relationship with God is a good place to start. I would like to admit that I don't have unforgiveness toward anyone, but it is taking daily surrender work to get there, and none of us do it perfectly. One of the things I have been practicing is telling people, "Thank you," even if they don't deserve it. This isn't natural, but over time, it has become a habit that helps me focus more on God's grace toward me than the offense. It is easy to forget that we represent Him in what can be a very rude, ungrateful, and entitled world sometimes, but we can walk in forgiveness with His grace.

I was recently reminded of how this works on a regular work morning as I was walking into a coffee shop. I graciously held the door open for a lady who was walking with her hands full of lattes, and she walked past me with an attitude through the door without saying thank you. As I mentioned her behavior to a friend, he reminded me that people aren't always aware of their behavior, and maybe her mind was preoccupied with something else. I have a pet peeve about inconsiderate behavior, specifically when it overlooks my kindness, but God used this and many other small incidences to help me understand that entitlement is not a part of the grace and forgiveness formula. The next day, I had to go shopping for clothing for my mom, who was traveling to a country with a cold climate, and because God has a sense of humor, He assigned Ms. Latte as the salesperson. She was very polite, helping me choose the right sizes and styles that fit my mom, which softened my heart, along with the words of my friend who encouraged me to forgive her for her action from the day before and believe the best. It is never fun being kind to unkind people, but it is possible when we change the way we see things.

The journey to victorious living has many twists and turns. Accepting God's grace makes life simple, but it is difficult for strong people who are always ready to help and are often afraid to show weakness. On the outside, we make life look put together and not so hard to manage, but on the inside, we are just as scared, tired, and hopeless as others who don't pretend to be strong all the time. Like a man-made dam, we have mastered the skill of holding in feelings and remaining calm during high-pressure situations, giving others permission to be weak, mourn, and excel. Because of this trait, people in leadership roles, specifically, must be intentional about allowing themselves to be collaborative and not have the answers all the time. There is so much freedom in admitting you don't know or, even better, letting someone else know for a change; showing this part of our humanity gives us opportunities to expand our way of doing things. Self-centered rigid thinking is also not a part of the grace-forgiveness formula. Jesus led His disciples with openness to recover from weakness and failure. Proverbs 24:16 (NKJV) says, "A righteous man may fall seven times And rise again, But the wicked shall fall by calamity." God's grace simplifies our time here on Earth amid all the setbacks and mistakes we experience. In His forgiveness, we are no longer guilty, and His love gives us the strength to overcome offenses quickly. This is good news for those of us who don't like asking for help and are still learning how to loosen up from a life filled with retribution. We can allow room for mistakes and repentance. Jesus is our example, and He didn't call us to a life of conditional love and acceptance. He is calling you to a victorious life, and it's time to answer.

CHAPTER 7

Load Shedding: "Saying Goodbye"

A space suit or spacesuit is a garment worn to keep a human alive in the harsh environment of outer space, vacuum, and temperature extremes. Space suits are often worn inside spacecraft as a safety precaution in case of loss of cabin pressure and are necessary for extravehicular activity (EVA), work done outside the spacecraft.[6]

As God exposes the capacity He placed in you for His work, He reduces the limitations that hold you back. This chapter was by far the most difficult to write. Loss was surrounding me, and it felt like pain consumed my life; my apprenticeship has ended with escaping, and I am becoming a seasoned veteran at facing life forward. Lately, I have been thinking about the purpose of seasons and how change is expected throughout our human experience to keep us constantly adapting. Within a

6 "Space Suit." Wikipedia, n.d. https://en.wikipedia.org/wiki/Space_suit.

few days, I will be leaving home for a month to undergo surgery to prevent vision loss. Leading up to the trip, I had to euthanize my dog and temporarily let go of my normal life by rearranging my finances, securing the house, and giving away my high-maintenance indoor plants. For the past three years, I've constantly been adapting to traumatic changes, feeling like my feet will never touch the ground. Astronauts have a similar experience maneuvering through their assignments in space, whether inside or outside the spacecraft; the feeling of being grounded probably doesn't return for months after they return to Earth.

I am about to walk into another uncontrollable situation; there will be surgeons and students watching as I am being probed and repaired while partially awake. The specific outcome is already known by God; my job is to be still and bravely allow change to unfold. Fortunately, unlike my first surgical experience, I won't be in a pandemic bubble, and I am surrounded by a stronger community that is helping me face the anxiety of these changes without focusing too much on what's next. I could ask God why I am experiencing so much difficulty at once, but it would be the same rhetorical question most of the world has been asking in this post-pandemic era. I feel like God is using the frequency of trauma to teach me how to lose control of outcomes. His grace is like the space suit, built for functionality and versatility to withstand change, and has kept me resiliently prepared for uncertainty.

"Because of the violence against your brother Jacob, you will be covered with shame; you will be destroyed forever" (Obadiah 1:10, NIV).

Obadiah was a prophet chosen by God to foretell the fate of Edom, the people of Esau, the brother who was deceived of his inheritance by Jacob (Israel), his younger brother. This resulted in years of conflict between the two nations; motivated by arrogance and pride, the Edomites allowed their hatred of Israel to consume them, which ultimately destroyed their future. If you've ever been deceived out of something that rightfully belonged to you (health, money, etc.), the temptation to retaliate with violence is always present; the difficulties of life, specifically the unfair ones, feel like intentional deception that can leave you asking why you should continue trusting in God for justice and what's in it for you. Esau wasted his future, his birthright meant nothing until he understood its value years later, but by that time, it was too late. Our lack of prudence has an echoing effect. Your rebellion could be alcoholism, which ruined your health and finances, or adultery, which ruined your marriage and family.

In my grieving, I made myself a promise to be angry but never let it consume me like it did in the past. As much as I hate sickness, death, and losing, facing those experiences helped me deal with the anger of losing more than anything else. They pointed me to God and made me more prudent about the simple acts we take for granted that have a tremendous impact on our life, like procrastination and apathy. We like to believe that everyone is inherently good deep down inside, but the Bible says in Jeremiah 17:9–10 (NIV),

> The heart is deceitful above all things and beyond cure. Who can understand it? "I the LORD search the heart and examine the mind, to reward each person according to their conduct, according to what their deeds deserve."

Humility is the deciding factor in God's economy of favor; it separates the meek from the proud and affects our legacy. Resisting anger when life is unfair takes courage. During recovery from surgery, my days included weekly trips back and forth to my doctor, taking medicine every two to three hours, managing intermittent pain, and battling adrenaline fatigue. At night, when my anxiety was at its worst, I cried, prayed, and begged God to help me get through the physical symptoms of fear as the pain became intense. One week after surgery, I woke up, and it was very difficult to see, a transient side effect. Ironically, it was during the week of Easter and the release of the movie The Journey, starring Andrea Bocelli. A popular opera singer who lost his sight at a younger age. I needed to get out of the room but even more so face the temporary setback with inspiration; as I sat watching him ride his horse with his family, talking about his faith, and living a full life, my terror disappeared. His courage helped me exchange my anger for praise as I realized holding on to fear only compounded an already stressful situation, so I decided to be grateful, believing that God would restore my losses, and even if He didn't, I could keep serving Him.

> Then Satan answered the LORD and said, "Skin for skin! All that a man has he will give for his life. But stretch out your hand and touch his bone and his flesh, and he will curse you to your face." And the LORD said to Satan, "Behold, he is in your hand; only spare his life."
>
> Job 2:4–6 (ESV)

Letting go of things that became a part of your stability in the process of change is progressive. To believe that God can give you better means giving up emotional and physical attachments over time; in fact, according to attachment theory research, in most cases, keeping a physical item of that person or thing helps us detach and grieve more safely. I was given a picture frame of my dog's paw print after she passed away, which helped me feel the pain of grief less and got me through the trauma of surgery. When I decided to let go of the medicine that provided me with security to accept the risk surrounding surgery, when I let go of people that no longer made me feel safe to accept the risk of being lonely for a while, along with losing my pet, that small commemorative gift represented the little stability I had left and kept me calm in the chaos. It's taught me never to judge how a person should grieve; the journey is deeply personal for everyone.

In this passage from Job, Satan assumed that Job would curse God when his health was attacked. It is the same superficial view we use to predict others' allegiance during life's unfairness because we cannot see the condition of their heart the way God can. After my condition improved, my doctor released me to travel back home with detailed instructions regarding my physical movements and a medicine routine for the next six weeks. Suddenly, I had to acknowledge that my life required simplicity, which meant permanent changes to my lifestyle.

A few days before my release, I was having doubts about changing the departure destination of my flight to attend an event God asked me to support before going home. I had attended the event in the past but was disappointed because I didn't receive the rewards that were promised. To get me there, I understood that my unmet expectations had to take a back seat to my obedience, so I bought my tickets and went without any preconceived notions. Without knowing it, a bad rainstorm and tornado threat would occur the day prior to my travel that flooded parts of the city and grounded all flights, which meant I would have been stranded if I didn't go along with God's plan. When I got to the other destination, God used me to inspire random strangers with my testimony about His grace during my difficulties and encouraged me to promote the event. I was learning the art of reframing. In psychology, cognitive reframing is a technique used to shift your mindset so you're able to look at a situation from a slightly different perspective, in this case, God's perspective. I decided to simply enjoy the diversion God was taking me on, which made me feel empowered and at ease. Knowing God is strategic, I embraced the lessons because I knew I would need blind trust for wherever He was taking me next. It's hard to see people, much less remember God's purpose, when life is that difficult. I became absorbed in my pain and wanted the real world to disappear, but it was not enough for me to continue wearing the badge of Christianity and nurse my grief in the comfort of my hotel room. God needed me in the field to express hope and courage in the face of chaos as an example of faith. Reading the Bible is easy and fun but is more challenging to live.

In the book of James 1:6–9, a double-minded man is explained to be unbalanced in all his ways; he is filled with insincerity and inconsistency, and he asks with doubt and suspicion. When I asked God why my desires were going unmet year after year, the Holy Spirit led me to this scripture. As I thought about the different areas of my life where I had one foot in and one foot out, I began to declare that I am learning to live a sincere and consistent lifestyle in chaos. God also used those forced changes and a diversion to shift me out of negative thinking that was activated by triggers that were pulling me back into the habit of self-pity He had already resolved. The hard work to lose the shell of hypervigilance that kept me guarded years before helps me throw caution to the wind regularly now. Most of my relationships have changed, I will never be comfortable with many norms again, and some material things are permanently gone, but I am more open to the new ways God is using to help me reach His destiny.

Maybe you're in a time of tremendous pain from constant losses, and God is asking you to change your plans and follow His lead, and you have doubts. He may be leading you to a place where you've experienced some disappointment in the past; one way you can move forward is by changing the way you see things. He is taking you there for a greater purpose; you are going there to help change something or someone.

Maybe someone will need to see what courage looks like in the face of uncertainty, and others will be there to simply give you the hug or smile of understanding you need. While I was experiencing overwhelming fear in recovery, I prayed that God would send people to show me hope and compassion; things we all need in large doses when life is unfair and unkind, but He did something better by helping me sow the seeds for the harvest I desired.

"Brethren, I do not count myself to have apprehended; but one thing I do, forgetting those things which are behind and reaching forward to those things which are ahead" (Philippians 3:13, NKJV).

Jesus spent most of His time surrounded by crowds and had to withdraw from people often to spend time with God and replenish His energy. The benefits of this rest and seclusion help the mind and body recharge and give us time to reassess our priorities; after years of looking for safety in my relationships, career, money, and independence, I am finding the power to feel safe was always inside of me. Perseverance to rest and let go is also involved in change. According to dictionary.com,[7] load shedding is the deliberate shutdown of electric power in a part or parts of a power-distribution system, generally to prevent the failure of the entire system when the demand strains the capacity of the system.

7 "Load-Shedding Definition & Meaning." Dictionary.com, n.d. https://www.dictionary.com/browse/loadshedding.

My mother is my greatest example of resilience; she spent over forty years of her life as an elementary school teacher and lived through a series of chronic traumatic life events but still managed to find humor in life. By the time I discovered that my life was severely out of balance, I had already wasted a lot of time, energy, and money on relationships and pursuits that slowed down my progress toward this mindset, but her response to life motivated me never to give up my ability to smile through pain or disappointment. I was an easy and difficult child because of my extremely quiet nature, but she allowed me to come out of my shell in my own time. Whether hot, cold, rainy, or windy, we know how to dress based on the weather; we learn to adapt to our external environment quickly but adapting to mental changes takes time and effort. If you struggle to believe in God's ability to help you get through the mental challenges that accompany loss, reflect on the times He delivered you in the past, and let the people around you that have already survived insurmountable pain renew your hope.

We can do all things through Christ, who strengthens us no matter how difficult life gets. John 10:10 talks about the abundant life He died for us to have. In our quest to live full lives, loss will always follow us, but so does goodness and mercy. Now that life is asking me to become lighter, I am deciding to reflect on a few things I need to let go of internally that are helping to increase my capacity for God. In the next few discourses, I want you to go with me on a psychological and spiritual analysis of the personal journey that helped me disengage from destructive habits that overloaded my life. I hope you can identify and, more importantly, find resolve.

Load 1—The Fixer

As a child, withdrawal wasn't restful for me; I used the time away from people to assess how I could fix or control narratives around me to circumvent the fear of rejection and abandonment. It was the only way I thought I could get attention and validation from others, but instead I became a fixer. One day, God showed me a picture of how this behavior was holding me and the people I interacted with in a cycle of victimhood.

I had signed up to participate in a charity event and volunteered to purchase items to give away. As I entered the drop-off point for donations and tried to engage a team member and friend, my presence was met with disdain. Clearly, he was not having a good day, a pattern I witnessed on several occasions but a behavior I had built up a false sense of grace for in myself and others. As I stood there, waiting with his back turned, no matter how much I tried to engage him, it was met with silent treatment one minute, and curt answers the next. The healed me had already learned how to deflect projected pain, but I remembered this behavior showing up frequently in my emotional patterns in the past and wanted to show compassion. To unlearn this behavior (known as protest in psychology), I had to learn how to use my words to express my feelings instead of acting them out. And it was a time I needed to allow my friend to do the same, so I continued my assignment and ignored his attention-seeking trap; our inability to communicate a negative feeling without projecting it onto others requires personal accountability.

Emotional manipulation, defined by WebMD, is when a manipulative person seeks power over someone else and employs dishonest or exploitative strategies to gain it. Unlike people in healthy relationships, which demonstrate reciprocity and cooperation, an emotional manipulator looks to use, control, or even victimize someone else. The root of this relational weakness can come from low self-esteem or being raised in an emotionally abusive environment, but it is never too late to learn social skills required for healthy interactions. And when you do, it's your responsibility to restore others. Galatians 6:1 (ESV), "Brothers, if anyone is caught in any transgression, you who are spiritual should restore him in a spirit of gentleness. Keep watch on yourself, lest you too be tempted." I did eventually graciously confront him about his behavior and, in time, noticed his interactions changing.

Load 2—Scarcity

As I reject substandard ways of living, I am learning how to let go of having just enough. There are some common untruths that we tell ourselves to sound spiritual, but it is fear-based thinking that limits our influence; for instance, being alive is enough, or I just want enough money to live comfortably. This thinking limits our ability to do more for ourselves, God, and others. The belief that being alive is enough has many people living untreated, unhealed, purposeless, and unhappy lives while a life filled with more-than-enough thinking seeks healing, is filled with purpose, and more hope to create positive change in the world. When this kind of thinking affects our spending, we accept debt as the norm, consume most of our resources selfishly, and give the bare minimum. To build a more purposeful life around God and community, giving of ourselves must become more sacrificial and honorable; God has more than enough to meet our needs, and when we evict just enough thinking from our mindset, He can trust us with more. Matthew 25:20–21 (NKJV),

> So he who had received five talents came and brought five other talents, saying, 'Lord, you delivered to me five talents; look, I have gained five more talents besides them.' His lord said to him, 'Well done, good and faithful servant; you

> were faithful over a few things, I will make you ruler over many things. Enter the joy of your lord.'

Load 3—Fear of Envy

> You desire but do not have, so you kill. You covet but you cannot get what you want, so you quarrel and fight. You do not have because you do not ask God. When you ask, you do not receive, because you ask with wrong motives, that you may spend what you get on your pleasures.
>
> James 4:2–3 (NIV)

Envy is the feeling of displeasure produced by witnessing or hearing of the advantage or prosperity of others; when you are targeted persistently by someone that is envious or antagonistic, you have the choice to shrink back or become more excellent. We either fight for pure self-preservation, flee to get away from a situation as soon as possible, freeze by pausing instead of running, or fawn to seek ways to neutralize the threat. Fawning was my way of dealing with envy because I didn't think what I had was enough. But once I gained the understanding that there is enough for everyone in God's economy (Psalm 145:16), having this fear became pointless. Envy will always be a part of the equation when you are making progress in any area of life; it is an insecurity you must ignore. We are encouraged to celebrate each other throughout the Word of God.

Growing up, I was intimated by competition and comparisons because of my shyness, but now that I have done a lot of work on healing my mentality, I can choose to be more collaborative in competitive environments. Envy disrupts the positive flow in relationships, and it slows down your path to getting things done; instead of being intimidated, refuse to accommodate it by becoming more excellent at being you. Psalm 23:4–5 (BSB),

> Even though I walk through the valley of the shadow of death, I will fear no evil, for You are with me; Your rod and Your staff, they comfort me. You prepare a table before me in the presence of my enemies.

Load 4—Proving

We all want to be rewarded for good work and should be, but there is no need to earn salvation through good works. I recognized proving had become a problem in my life when I got rejected by social groups; we've all been there. We dress our best, flatter, and hang on to their every move only to be turned down flat. We often try to do the same when relating to God, but Ephesians 2:8–9 (NIV) reminds us, "For it is by grace you have been saved, through faith—and this is not from yourselves, it is the gift of God—not by works, so that no one can boast." Receiving the gift of forgiveness and right standing with God is accomplished by our faith in Jesus; there is no other way (John 14:6). It's natural to feel overwhelming pride when we do great things for God, but they are not indicators of someone's right standing with Him. Sadly, there are many people that love God and preach His Word but do not have a committed relationship with Him. God loves relating with us and honors what He can with us more than our achievements or status; we should all strive to be seen in our relationships, not as an opportunity but as a person worthy of love and serving because we love. John 3:16 (BSB), "For God so loved the world that He gave His one and only Son, that everyone who believes in Him shall not perish but have eternal life."

Load 5—Entitlement

> Then Nathan said to David, "You are that man! This is what the LORD, the God of Israel, says: 'I anointed you king over Israel, and I delivered you from the hand of Saul. I gave your master's house to you, and your master's wives into your arms. I gave you the house of Israel and Judah. And if all this has been too little, I would have given you even more.'"
>
> 2 Samuel 12:7–8 (NIV)

At some point, we all must face up to our part in bad consequences. Before I decided to start showing up in my relationships with flaws and imperfections, I struggled with an entitlement mentality. According to WebMD, entitlement may be due to social factors like the environment you grew up in, the way your parents treated you, whether adults solved your problems for you, or how you are treated by authority figures. Our emotions and sexuality are two of our highest forms of human intimacy and often the most misused, but giving the Holy Spirit access to these parts of our life and taming our senses helps us with healthy boundaries.

In life, most people who struggle with a rejected past have a problem with entitlement. Have you ever caught yourself acting like the rules should be modified to suit you often? The store is a minute away from closing, but you're a regular customer, so they should let you in; someone parked in your space, so you sent out a warning email to everyone in your work group. If there is a rule, you want it to be enforced because someone always must pay when you are being inconvenienced. I roll my eyes at people like this, but this form of pride is common. If you've experienced prolonged rejection as you gain better positions in life, an entitlement mentality can result in excessive and harmful behaviors if you don't practice delayed gratification and putting the needs of others first regularly. One day, I decided to take God with me on a shopping trip to purchase clothes for work, and He asked me to purchase a top that I didn't really like, so I left it. When I got home, I kept thinking, *But God really liked it. Even if I don't, I can buy it just because He did.* In the same way, we can delay having what we want when we want it to please God in other areas of our life.

Load 6—Fear of Authority

Abuse of authority is an unfortunate reality we all experience throughout life; it is unacceptable for any person to use his or her position of power to manipulate, dominate, and intimidate others, but this kind of behavior is tolerated and even praised in many relationships, organizations, and cultures. From a familial perspective, some children are taught never to question authority, and when taken to an extreme, some biblical theories support the notion of the unquestionable and unapproachable nature of authority figures, even God. But Proverbs 29:25 (NKJV) says, "The fear of man brings a snare, But whoever trusts in the LORD shall be safe," and we are also encouraged to seek and ask. We grow in our understanding of this when we detach from fear-based tactics that cause fear of retribution when communicating with authority figures, having a manager, parent, and, more importantly, a God that you can trust in ways that do not violate personal choice is safe. God's way of relating with humanity is a blueprint of how authority figures should lead. Abuse should never be tolerated. Rules and laws should be followed but not at the expense of an individual's safety and the right to be heard; it's a lesson we all must learn to maintain healthy boundaries. Mutual love and respect in relationships require an attitude of reciprocity. My healthy view of authority was restored when I began to see the empowering nature of God.

First John 4:4 (KJV), "Ye are of God, little children, and have overcome them: because greater is he that is in you, than he that is in the world."

Luke 10:19–20 (KJV), "Behold, I give unto you power to tread on serpents and scorpions, and over all the power of the enemy: and nothing shall by any means hurt you."

Exodus 15:2 (ESV), "The Lord is my strength and my song, and he has become my salvation; this is my God, and I will give him praise, my father's God, and I will exalt him."

Deuteronomy 31:6 (KJV), "Be strong and of a good courage, fear not, nor be afraid of them: for the Lord thy God, he it is that doth go with thee; he will not fail thee, nor forsake thee."

Load 7—Impatience

How we use time is more advantageous when we do the right things at the right time, as we have limits to our productivity based on gender, age, and quality of life. Global research and statistics reveal that women have a greater life expectancy rate than men, yet according to the American Psychological Association, one in four women acknowledge they are not doing enough when it comes to managing stress, but only 17 percent of men feel this way. The seventh hang-up I am working to eliminate from my lifestyle is impatience; it steals time and depletes resources, energy, and money. As I get older, my type A personality is slowly disappearing, and I am learning to fight less with God as I wake up to noisy joints and occasionally surprised by grey hair.

My stress management technique was getting everything done quickly, but life has been constantly slowing me down. If God has given you the vision to achieve a few things that are outside of your element that will require some training, impatience must go. I have always had a teachable attitude, but hastiness was causing avoidable mistakes and creating an inability to retain important facts in the learning process. To give me more advanced training in patience, God answered my prayer for a new puppy after I lost my dog. Like a baby, they require a lot of attention and keep you on your feet; I had to increase my workout routine just to keep up with him. Adjusting my lifestyle to accommodate his training has been fun but brutal. I named him Maximus, after the gladiator, without taking it seriously. In three months, he has destroyed a few toys, potty pads, and shoes, escaped his playpen a few times, attempted to chew through several power chords, and I've caught him fighting the wall several times. Obedience training has been a nightmare sometimes, but he's also an affectionate, kind dog, which makes my work of patience more gratifying.

A lighter life means ending relationships, habits, and thinking that no longer fit your life. There is no scarcity in God; He is a God of abundance that wants His best for us, not what we feel is His best, but what He knows is best. Change is inevitable when our values no longer align with the expectations of others. When our safety and identity become more grounded in Christ, insecurities that once controlled our decisions lose power.

As a child, my greatest fear was letting my parents down; I always made sure I was doing the right thing to impress them even if I was unhappy, but when I became a woman, having to learn how to find safety within myself and God meant reparenting myself. Detaching from these loads of insecurity took years of saying yes and no to how I truly felt, and no matter how much it hurt someone else, if it aligned with God's purpose and identity, I learned to let go. Unlearning how to make decisions based on your truth alone will involve many difficult decisions and disheartening conversations between you and God. The day I typed the first word of this testimony, I said goodbye to the part of myself that desperately needed the approval of others; I resigned from doing and proving my way through life and began enjoying it. I give up apologizing and explaining myself to people that had already decided to misunderstand me; I allow more room for others that accept me just as I am to enter my life.

Writing about this part of my life felt like an essay filled with self-deprecating stories at times, but I was willing to let my failures and successes speak as a witness to what facing life with and without God is like. There is no comfort or resting place for insecurity in a life that is surrendered to God. When you are pushing your way through the hardness of life, see change as a step into freedom and a future filled with new adventures. I am happy that God never let my feet touch the ground until I found my way home, and you, too, can keep going after failure, disappointment, and regret. Never be afraid to start over.

> "Sing, barren woman, you who never bore a child; burst into song, shout for joy, you who were never in labor; because more are the children of the desolate woman than of her who has a husband," says the LORD. "Enlarge the place of your tent, stretch your tent curtains wide, do not hold back; lengthen your cords, strengthen your stakes."
>
> Isaiah 54:1–2 (NIV)

CHAPTER 8

Mission Complete: "It's Okay! Come Outside"

When a spacecraft such as the Space Shuttle leaves orbit and reenters the atmosphere (Earth) as it travels to a landing site, there is a critical period of time when all communications between the spacecraft and the ground are lost. This phenomenon is due to the tremendous heating experienced by the craft during reentry and is termed "reentry blackout."[8]

A few years ago, I watched an interview of an NFL player talking about his transition to Christianity and how he had to stay outside the team huddle intentionally sometimes to avoid the aggressive language that was involved in game strategy before a play. When we surrender our heart to God, we automatically become sensitive to some things and find it easy to give them

8 "Spacecraft Reentry Communications Blackout." Space Academy, n.d. http://www.spaceacademy.net.au/spacelink/blackout.htm.

up. When I found it very hard to be in the same place doing the same things with the same people, it felt like I woke up as a different person inside; the person I used to be had left, and I couldn't recognize who I had become. In the book of John 15:1–4 (NIV), Jesus explains the process of pruning, cutting away dead things that hinder growth in the process of change.

> I am the true vine, and my Father is the gardener. He cuts off every branch in me that bears no fruit, while every branch that does bear fruit he prunes so that it will be even more fruitful. You are already clean because of the word I have spoken to you. Remain in me, as I also remain in you. No branch can bear fruit by itself; it must remain in the vine. Neither can you bear fruit unless you remain in me.

"The fruit of the Spirit is love, joy, peace, patience, kindness, goodness, faithfulness, gentleness, self-control" (Galatians 5:22, ESV). In times of pruning, we draw closer to God to develop more of these Christ-like character traits for spiritual maturing and to influence positive change in the people connected to us. As the fruit of God's Spirit grows in us, over time, we lose even more interest in certain behaviors, people, and environments. In gardening, pruning not only removes dead things to allow room for new growth but also protects your property from damage that can be caused by dead branches and debris. Remember that fun friend that you used to talk to for hours, that always knew where all the great parties were, that started boring you to tears? He or she represents something that needs to be cut away to maybe develop the fruit of self-control within you; it doesn't feel good at the moment, but later, we appreciate God not asking our permission to remove us from some people and places.

The shuttle requires thermal protection to withstand the extreme heat as it reenters Earth's atmosphere. When God equips us with gifts that are surrendered for His use, we usually experience many difficulties to test our fruit as we arrive at the opportunities assigned to us. Imagine an important client trying to get a word in during a negotiation with that chatty fruit that rubbed off on you from your friend. My job requires a lot of listening and talking; by the end of the day, I appreciate the silence of not having to talk. Pruning is also God's way of eliminating norms that drain our energy and shift our focus.

After my dog was euthanized, I didn't realize how much her cancer treatments had taken over both of our lives; for over a year, my finances and energy were rapidly depleting as I was trying to maintain a full-time job, write a book, and recover physically from trauma. Sometimes God must take away things from us that we refuse to believe have ended or are ending; when I think about God's way of transitioning us, pain and loss are always part of the equation. As I stood there comforting my dog while she slipped away, I felt a sudden overwhelming feeling of emptiness and a new beginning all at once; our routine was gone forever. Who was going to meet me at the door every time I returned home? It was a sound I had been accustomed to for fourteen years. I knew my life was changing traumatically but didn't know how to face it. After witnessing my sister's death, I thought I was strong enough to handle letting her go, but this time it was different. I had never allowed myself to love something that deep before and had overlooked the fact that she had become a child to me; it was the first time I let myself feel the physical pain of a broken heart without trying to minimize it.

In the days that followed, I had to repeat the fact that she was gone every time I was reminded of our routine and gave myself permission to cry whenever I needed. I promised not to let the sadness consume me by allowing my feelings to surface and talk about them, even if only to myself. Throughout the Psalms, David expressed his varying emotions with God in what he often referred to as the secret place, where he was hidden from life's difficulties with regret and resolve. It's the space in our hearts that's reserved to express how we really feel and get brutally honest about how angry, scared, or disappointed life feels to a God we know listens and understands. He does not disappear when we cling to our vices either; He wants us to ask for help when we are in the middle of acting out our fears. Every person that suffered a great deal of trauma and managed to survive with their sanity intact is familiar with this part of the grieving process.

Pruning is the most difficult part of the Christian walk because you can't skip steps. Life seemed more carefree and lighter before I decided to obey God; my voice wasn't being heard for the right reasons, my heart was closed off, and there were fewer opportunities to feel hurt deeply, but the tradeoff was far better. When reading the psalms of David, empathy arises as you feel understanding surface through his expressions about defeat and victory. As I walked through the grieving process of losing a pet, it was the pet owners and parents of children that reached out more to check on me; they were the ones that understood me wanting to get another dog sooner rather than later. God's ever-present help gives us the understanding and compassion we need to face the pruning times in our lives along with the community around us.

When I was a little girl, my grandmother woke up every morning around 5:00 a.m. to pray; she prayed for people all over the world, which was very confusing to me. I didn't understand her reasoning until I learned more about her life story. She had seen many losses and painful events in her life, but instead of choosing loneliness in her suffering, she had compassion for others that might be suffering in the same way or worse. In this safe space, we give God room to melt any hardness from the pain that exists in our hearts as He shows us the suffering of others to give us hope and courage to rebound. It's not easy to let go of things we loved for a long time. When the pain of holding on led me to surrender, my compassion for others grew stronger.

"And I will restore to you the years that the locust hath eaten, the cankerworm, and the caterpiller, and the palmerworm, my great army which I sent among you" (Joel 2:25, KJV).

During the summer months in the Bahamas, we are prepared for hurricane season and load-shedding activities that result in frequent electricity disruptions; as the winter approaches, we breathe a sigh of relief and begin to recover after these threats have passed. Summertime is also a time of harvest, and whatever is lost is reinvested during planting time in the fall and spring months. After I couldn't picture my life without a dog, I downloaded a picture of a puppy for my vision board. As I was purchasing the last bag of dog food, I mentioned to the cashier that I was interested in a puppy. Within a few days before the euthanized appointment, without knowing the description I had in mind, she sent me a video of a puppy that looked exactly like the one I wanted. I was in shock, thinking it was too good to be true, but it wasn't. Can God really work that fast on our desires? Yes, He can and wants to restore that quickly. In this passage of Joel, God was promising restoration after great devastation over the land of Judah; everything was consumed, but God extended mercy because of His love for them. I didn't think I deserved another pet that soon, but I prayed and believed for it; it is so hard for us to believe God wants to be good to us after chaos that we even sometimes count our losses without believing recovery is possible. When the answers come, are you prepared to receive them graciously? God wants to restore your losses; He wants us to win, and even if it feels too good to be true, receive it with gratitude. To believe that a relationship, place, thing, or opportunity could be restored, you first have to picture it in your mind, then your hand, declare it, and eventually, you'll possess it. I never thought it was that easy, but it can be.

Recovery plans require strategies to help us exit and reset in life transitions smoothly; our vision becomes more focused and defined when we see the way forward. Seeing a new dog gave me the courage to let go of the sick dog; before I exited my last job, a part of my exit strategy was to buy the company car that was not for sale at the time; it was purchased brand new, and I was the only driver. I prayed and believed without making any formal request to the company, and within a few months, management decided they no longer wanted to maintain cars as assets and sold them. It was the motivation God knew I needed to move on. What motivations do you need for the exit and recovery God and life are asking of you?

I find nothing more satisfying than seeing a plan come together. When it's time to move on, if it's a strategy that you need, God will help you plan it by putting desires and dreams in your heart. Knowing you have an out and a vision for what's next when things are ending gives you more patience with the annoyances and adversity involved in your present circumstances; directives that once annoyed you will roll off your shoulders when the exit is defined, and the value of things that you once held so tightly depreciate quickly. During the time between your imagination and reality, the devil will set a few traps to create disbelief, anything to prevent you from having anything that matches God's will for your life. The chaos I experienced from the time God placed becoming a writer in my vision until now was planned by the devil as I was planting, but instead of stopping me, they motivated me to go further; the enemy is expecting a harvest in your life, and he knows

God's deep love for you. Life circumstances may have destroyed some of your possessions, but when you have a positive outlook, there is still hope.

> Listen carefully to my speech, And to my declaration with your ears. See now, I have prepared my case, I know that I shall be vindicated. Who is he who will contend with me? If now I hold my tongue, I perish.
>
> Job 13:17–19 (NKJV)

Job was holding on to his faith in God to avenge him while he was mocked for his unwavering hope. To trust the same God that allowed Satan to attack you is irrational; Job had every right to seek revenge as he was surrounded by terrible losses and pessimists, but instead of hatred, he chose love. In a scene from Batman Begins years after the murder of his parents, Bruce Wayne wanted to avenge their deaths by convincing himself that justice and revenge are the same, but his friend had to explain that justice is about harmony while revenge is about making yourself feel better. It is a blessing to have people in your life that will tell you the truth when you're in pain; their honesty gives you the courage to try again. In contrast, the pessimist will either cuddle you or encourage you to give up, but Job had the internal strength and wisdom he needed to confront their negativity with prayer and faith.

Jesus instructs us to seek justice through harmony in the same way in scriptures like Matthew 5:43–48. Praying for people that speak against you helps prune pride and anger, which poisons our attitude and reinforces discord in our relationships, but when we let go of blame, our focus shifts from issues to solutions, and we can receive God's instructions more calmly and confidently. Over the course of my life, I have walked away from a few attractive opportunities that seemed rational but were not suitable for me; then, there were other circumstances that were not as exciting and difficult but where I needed to stay. In both scenarios, the one constant was my faith to trust that God knew all the answers. One day, I reached out to a friend who had switched business locations, but God gave me clear instructions not to go; she's very professional and does a great job, and I thought, What's the big deal? God said, "You'll see." I discovered that the owner of the property was someone from my past that attacked me verbally and financially, so I had to cut ties with my new friend completely.

In other scenarios, I had to learn how to navigate environments where He needed me to stay but separate myself from certain groups within organizations. The courage to make relational adjustments has always been a challenge for me, but as my faith matures, I am learning how to minimize offenses and keep safe boundaries with others while following God's guidance.

Refusing to let yourself become bitter from persecution is a choice, even if you cannot see the silver lining. Believe that God knows best and celebrate the blind spots as His protection. Life is never all bad. As we process through the peaks and valleys of change, exalting love keeps our hearts open to God's provision. Job understood this. As we grow and change, our choice to remain harmonious will only offend those that have no hope for recovery. Abide in His love.

God's deep love and attachment to Israel is a depiction of His grace toward the misplaced, unheard, and unseen; He repetitively expresses Himself as their place of safety and abundance. Our peace and happiness begin with how we see ourselves through the eyes of God, how He feels about us, and His design for our lives despite imperfections and failures. As the Lord rearranged the desires of my heart to align with His, I gave up a load of guilt I had carried around for years exhausting myself with work to meet standards I believed I needed to feel validated. A few weeks ago, I surprised myself by not doing something immediately to address the weight gain I was experiencing from comfort eating and not being able to do high-intensity workouts after surgery. The positive effect of uncontrollable change is you care less about impressing people and learn to have more grace for yourself. What if you never get married or stay married? What if you never achieve another big thing in your career or personal life? Is the gift of being complete within enough? We all must ask what-if questions after trauma teach us what's important. We stop living pretentious lives and begin to flow with changes in peace.

If you struggle with apathy, low self-worth, and identity issues, allow the Holy Spirit to help you do the internal work of rebuilding courage and good character while resetting your life. Our uniqueness is not an enigma, God cares more about our wholeness than our status in society, and He wants to hold a deep, intimate place in our hearts that keeps us secure in this fact. There are caring, impactful people in the world, and I am trying to do my part daily without becoming an imposter again. This is a message I repeat to myself every time I think I am not doing enough or connecting with the wrong people; we are only meant to match perfectly through this world by God's grace. Being that right person based on our identity in Christ while working on our life purpose with God and allowing healing consistently keeps us moving perfectly in an imperfect world.

> The next day as they were leaving Bethany, Jesus was hungry. Seeing in the distance a fig tree in leaf, he went to find out if it had any fruit. When he reached it, he found nothing but leaves, because it was not the season for figs. Then he said to the

> tree, "May no one ever eat fruit from you again."
> And his disciples heard him say it.
>
> Mark 11:12–14 (NIV)

There are several options to alter your body into whatever is trending as cool and acceptable, having the right fashion sense is no longer enough to fit in or increase influence in our society; the pressure to maintain relevance due to social media has increased focus on the superficial exponentially. Jesus was persuaded that fruit was present on the fig tree based on the appearance of leaves. Having substance with the right appearance will take you further than having a good image alone; it is very disappointing to invest in anything beautiful that cannot produce results, whether it's a product, service, person, or opportunity. I believe the same displeasure Jesus had for this tree that had not produced fruit is the same for anyone that possesses gifts or talents that are not advancing His goodness on the earth. Jesus proceeded to curse the fig tree, and the next day, it was found dried up from the roots. His purpose was to demonstrate how the power of words spoken in faith directly to a problem eliminates the root and its symptoms.

No matter how much you enhance your physical beauty or improve your financial status or material possessions, if the root of your problems is not addressed, your life will not change permanently. We all have used human love, things, or achievement to fix the internal crisis of the heart when emotions are too difficult to face, we make a lot of mistakes, and God still accepts us. It's never too late to simplify and reassess your lifestyle by going beyond the superficial to face the deep issues removing one layer at a time. When I became conscious of fractures in my communication that made me fail constantly in relationships, I hired a life coach and invested in whatever I needed to learn how to become better. In the book Attached by Amir Levine and Rachel Heller, people with a secure attachment style know how to communicate their own expectations and respond to their partners needs effectively without having to resort to protest behavior such as leaving the room in the middle of a disagreement or playing mind games to get attention. During our prayer time, we can surrender our insecurities with no shame; this helped me learn how to communicate my feelings and have the courage to resolve conflict. When was the last time you ignored a phone call or busyness, looked your children, spouse, friend, or stranger in the eyes, and really listened without interrupting? Can you commit to the work it requires to be better? I believe we all can with God's help and when we are ready to change.

According to LinkedIn, children who can attract and maintain eye contact and therefore increase attention have the best chance of being fed and cared for. Whatever dysfunction you recognize in your communication pattern, it can be unlearned, and you can retrain your mind to react differently. Levine and Heller explain that attachment principles teach us that most people are only as needy as their unmet needs. When their emotional needs are met, and the earlier, the better, they usually turn the emotions outward, which is defined as the dependency paradox; the more effectively dependent people are on one another, the more independent and daring they become. I experienced this first-hand the morning I was leaving for work and encountered a stranger parked behind me as I locked my gate; he proceeded to stare and then drove off slowly. When I got back into my car, instead of panicking, I called a friend and spoke to a police officer and my neighbors; it was a lot of telling, but I needed to feel safe and grounded again. That evening, instead of locking the doors early, I carried on as if nothing happened with a feeling of safety because I had people looking out for me. When your capacity to feel safe independently is challenged, it is always better to seek help sooner rather than later, and God can lead you to the right resources to help you become the interdependent person He made you to be. Don't be afraid to go beyond the surface; get to know your neighbors if you don't, and research until you find a good physician or therapist if that's what you need.

God wants to lead you to where the nutrients are for the fruit He wants to produce in your life.

> Wake up! Strengthen what remains and is about to die, for I have found your deeds unfinished in the sight of my God. Remember, therefore, what you have received and heard; hold it fast, and repent. But if you do not wake up, I will come like a thief, and you will not know at what time I will come to you.
>
> Revelation 3:2–3 (NIV)

I was asked to find a way to get medical supplies to a close family member who left the country for an extended period, but the only option was to find someone who was traveling. I had no idea how it would happen, but I collected all the supplies and packaged as if God had already handpicked a person for me that week. After exhausting all my contacts, I became hopeless, but just when I was about to give up, a friend called and said she knew someone who was willing to take the supplies for me at no cost. My faith, although strong and imperfect, gave me access to God's provision based on my ability to overlook the impossible by preparing and then acting without any physical evidence. Having a reputation as someone who knows how to get things done is great. God loves to see our faith in action. The church of Sardis, which is referred to as the dead church, felt established in having a good reputation but didn't work diligently on the condition of their hearts. Getting the job done is half the battle.

To see continued growth in your relationship with God, you have to allow His Word to change the defects of your heart. It can be as simple as dropping your pride and letting Him help you work on having a better attitude, discipline your words, or showing more respect for authority; all these solutions can be found in His Word. Sardis is instructed to strengthen what remains and is about to die. I usually keep my Bible next to my bed like most people, but I cried, worried, and remained clueless night after night, searching the internet about how to address specific problems. But when I decided to open the Bible consistently every morning, my life began to change. What therapy couldn't heal in months, the words of the Bible did as I learned to read it slowly and ponder it throughout the day; it showed me parts of myself that I couldn't see and the things I ignored.

The Scripture warns that those who hear and refuse to live out what is instructed in the Word of God habitually will be caught off guard when the Lord returns due to their apathy. Apathy is insidious; it happens as we focus more on daily obligations, and our time for spiritual renewal is left dormant or given a glance every now and then. In my free time, I love to watch professional football and basketball, especially during the playoffs; if a team plays a highly defensive series with a short recovery period, it is more challenging for them to compete against a more well-rested opponent in the next round. The probability of losing increases more if the opponent is well-organized and consistent. As I reset and simplify my lifestyle, the slow pace revealed how going fast for too long depleted my ability to carry out my spiritual assignments more than any other area of my life. To recover, I started to develop tunnel vision about my lifestyle choices by shifting my focus from whatever was distracting me as soon as I recognized it.

Your recovery may look the same or different, but at some point, breaking familial, cultural, and societal norms permanently is required to improve the progress of growth in our lives. I spent most of my life in the driver's seat, but now I am learning to enjoy the view from the passenger seat, and noticing all the buildings and corners I couldn't see before. When we become grounded, our desire for wonder returns, and we can see new ways of doing things, learn about life at a steady pace, and loosen the tight grip on how things should be. There is so much hope and joy in knowing this kind of life can exist in a world filled with so much uncertainty and pressure to achieve all we can. Progressing toward maturity, we tend to leave parts of ourselves ignored and unhealed.

As children, we've all experienced a time when we got lost or weren't picked up on time; it was lonely, and time seemed endless; that child is still inside most of us. Some are still waiting to be rescued, while others have already found safety. In one of my recent counseling sessions, I was asked what I would say to the little girl inside of me, the one I ignored all those years that was still waiting to be seen and chosen. Without hesitation, I thought, It's okay! Come outside. I pictured myself bending down, taking her hand, and leading her out of those gates of fear that denied her access to a life rich with possibilities, walking past broken dreams and promises, not knowing where we would end up but being fully convinced that we could no longer remain in obscurity. I was walking her home to safety, where our identity in Christ exists. He is giving us everything we need; He understands us and promises that the feeling of aloneness will never be found again. I have faith to believe you can do the same for yourself.

"In this the love of God was manifested toward us, that God has sent His only begotten Son into the world, that we might live through Him" (1 John 4:9, NKJV).

Declarations

Identity

God only created one me, my path is unique, and I belong.

The truth of who I am is in Christ, not my past. That was then; this is now.

I am a new creation in Christ; old things have passed away, and behold, all things are new.

The truth of who I am is in Christ, not a position, person, or thing.

I am confident of this; God, who began a good work in me, will carry it out to completion until the day of Christ Jesus.

I value God's opinion of me more than the opinion of anyone else.

I am fearfully and wonderfully made in the image and likeness of God.

I have the same mind in me that Christ has towards me.

Where the Spirit of the Lord is, there is liberty. I, with unveiled face, beholding in a mirror the glory of the Lord is being transformed into that same image from glory to glory just as by the Spirit of the Lord.

I stand fast, therefore, in the liberty by which Christ has made me free and will not be entangled again with a yoke of bondage.

Emotions

The joy of the Lord is my strength.

God has turned my mourning into dancing and my sorrow into joy.

Emotions matter; hope deferred makes the heart sick.

I treat myself with kindness, compassion, and understanding.

No more will my eyes grow weak with sorrow or fail because of my enemies.

God has strengthened my weak hands and made steady my feeble knees.

A wise head has a still tongue, but a fool gives full vent to his feelings.

I am quick to hear, slow to speak, and slow to wrath.

The perfect love of God has cast out fear of intimacy and success from my heart.

Bitterness and grudges will not serve as my necklace, nor will worry or depression cover me like a garment.

Because I have made the Lord my refuge, and the Most High is my dwelling, no plague will overtake me, no disaster will come near me.

For He will command His angels concerning me to guard me in all my ways; they will lift me up in their hands so that I will not strike my foot against a stone.

The wicked flee when no man pursues, but the righteous are as bold as a lion.

I am worthy of being loved and giving love; my acceptance is based on the love of Christ, not my performance.

Promotion comes from God, not man.

I have the power, love, and a sound mind to walk away from unsafe situations and maintain my peace.

I will not minimize or be conceited about the blessings God has given me out of fear.

Loneliness and self-pity will not disrupt my healing process. With God's strength, I will never go back to people, places, or habits that devalue me.

I am emotionally available, open, and honest about who I am and what I am feeling.

I am blessed with a humble attitude to take responsibility when I am wrong and admit to my mistakes.

Health & Safety

My eyes will not dim, nor will my natural force depart from me.

I shall not die but live and declare the works of the Lord.

Jesus was wounded for my transgressions, crushed for my iniquities; upon Him was the chastisement that brought me peace, and by His stripes, I am healed.

The Lord will turn the counsel of all those that conspire evil and harm against me and my family into foolishness.

In peace, I will lie down and sleep, for you alone, Lord, make me dwell in safety.

On the day of my trouble, I will call upon God, and He will answer me.

There are more people that show up for me than those that are against me.

Mind and body, you are safe and loved; I will see disaster no more.

Body, I love and respect you all the time. Thank you for working hard for me.

The Lord guides me continually, satisfies my desire in scorched places, and makes my bones strong; I am like a watered garden, like a spring of water whose waters do not fail.

I am a good steward and cheerful giver of the time, money, and resources God trusts me to manage.

Boundaries

I trust God's timing and remain still.

I forgive quickly and trust slowly.

No weapon formed against me should prosper, and every tongue that rises up against me in judgment shall be condemned.

The prudent foresees danger and flees, but fools pass on and are punished.

I am teachable and give up the need to know everything.

I am blessed with the courage never to be shy, afraid of being judged, or isolate myself in self-pity.

The fear and insecurity in others do not belong to me.

I accept people for who they are and not what I want them to be.

I am blessed with a humble attitude to take responsibility when I am wrong and admit to my mistakes.

I understand where my responsibility begins and ends in my relationships.

When I was a child, I spoke as a child, and I acted as a child, but now that I am an adult, I put away childish things.

I stand fast in the liberty that Christ has made me free.

I am no longer in bondage to replicating trauma and pain.

The fear of man and rejection no longer exist in my nature.

I live within healthy boundaries and respect the free will of others; love is a choice.

I do not violate my conscience; I know how to resolve conflicts without aborting divine connections.

I do not isolate myself to seek my own desire.

I embrace wise counsel in relationships and the guidance of the Holy Spirit.

I know how to give the advantage without being misused in my relationships.

Printed in the USA
CPSIA information can be obtained
at www.ICGtesting.com
LVHW010012220124
769280LV00003B/188

9 798890 414571